VICTORIOUS

A Strategic Guide To Everyday Living

Matthew & Siobhan Oliver

Matthew & Siobhan Oliver
The Family Church
1529 Eureka Road, Suite 110
Roseville, CA 95661

Scripture quotations (unless otherwise noted) are taken from:

The Holy Bible, New International Version, NIV, Copyright 1973, 1978, 1984, 2011, Biblica, Inc.

The Holy Bible, New Living Translation, Copyright 1996, by Tyndale Charitable Trust

The Holy Bible, The New King James, Copyright 1982 by Thomas Nelson, Inc.

ISBN-13: 978-1986821797
ISBN-10: 198682179X

THANK YOU

Two little words that never fully express the magnitude of their meaning. Our names are on the front of the cover, but the pages within hold the insight, brilliance, revelations and understanding of a powerful team, an amazing community, true friends and family. We can write, but to make it coherent and beautiful took countless hours and investment from those we are honored to call friends.

Thank You to Kristine Dohner for her willingness to sacrifice so much to see another's dream become a reality. And Thank You to Dennis Dohner for loaning your wife away for hours to make this happen, and for your encouragement to live victoriously. Thank You to Deb Hollis for stepping up and owning this vision, for encouraging us to write… and write… and write some more. I am honored to have you as part of this team and this family. And Neal, thanks for letting her play. Thank You, Auston Oliver, for your design brilliance and creativity and for having awesome parents! And Kiley, thanks for marrying him.

You are only as strong as your team, and the whole team at Family made this possible. They have contributed in more ways than they will ever truly know and are living *victoriously*. Jordan and Kelsey, Thank You for not letting us settle, ever. Tara and Mike, Thank You for amazing friendship, encouragement, and for being willing to challenge us. Renee and Dave, Thank You for huge hearts and loving outrageously. Sharon and Jay, Thank You guys for showing us how to believe in each other. Christina, you work hard behind the scene, but you are vital to this team. Thank You for being an important part.

As a whole, Thank You to the Family Church. Partnered with you in what God has called us to, we are living the victory and declaring to the region around us and to the world that in Christ we are Victorious.

CONTENTS

Acknowledgments   i

Introduction   v

How Do I Use This Book?   ix

Challenge 1: Winning Matters   1

Challenge 2: Pray Like it Matters   9

Challenge 3: Old Dogs, New Tricks   17

Challenge 4: How Hungry Are You?   27

Challenge 5: Don't Settle for the Miracle When You Have a Promise   33

Challenge 6: Whose Light is Shining?   41

Challenge 7: God Bless You   49

Challenge 8: Listen   55

Challenge 9: Remember Me   61

Challenge 10: Power Must Look Powerful   67

Challenge 11: The Power of Confidence   79

Challenge 12: In The Midnight Hour   87

Challenge 13: The Power of Presence   95

Challenge 14: Fully Restored   101

Challenge 15: Get Your Hopes Up   109

Challenge 16: You've Got What You Need   117

Challenge 17: More   127

Challenge 18: The Power of Favor   135

Challenge 19: A New Thing   141

Challenge 20: Pursuit   149

Challenge 21: Your Victory   155

About the Authors   162

INTRODUCTION

It all started with a very common question. "How are you doing today?" It is the same question we hear all the time. I have probably been asked a thousand times, "How are you doing today?" There are so many answers, so many possibilities. But my response was simple, "Victorious!"

Well, not really. Not that often. It was not how I felt, how I looked, not how my day was going, and not how my life was going. But it's what you say, what people expect to hear, it's what we are supposed to say.

That's how it all started.

Someone asked me how I was doing and I told them what they wanted to hear, or maybe what I wish the truth was, "Victorious!" That's when the challenge started. It was then that God began to show me, reveal to me, what a victorious life looks like.

We are called to live victoriously. Jesus gave us the victory. If you have been in church long enough you know all the bumper sticker phrases that we have been taught, "We don't war for victory, we war from victory." What does that even mean? We say it and we move on, without ever really experiencing it. Not me, not any more. If I have something, I want to understand what it is, how it works, and how it should look in my life. If I have victory, I don't want to just say it, I want to experience it, feel it, live it and showcase it in my life.

God began to reveal to me understanding about victory. Victory, always comes at a price. The price is battle. The price is war. In real life all wars have casualties. In our personal life the casualties of war for victory may include fear, doubt, worry, or poverty. The price to pay for those casualties is tough - patience, forgiveness, peace. This happy word, *victorious*, that I threw around lightly is a powerful word in the Kingdom. Every victory is a result of a battle.

God was asking me if I really wanted to be victorious. If so, was I suited up for battle? Was I ready to fight on behalf of those victories? Did I even understand the value of what that victory would mean in my life? Or was I simply looking for the plunder of the win? Yes, there can be amazing plunder, resources, and valuable commodities after a win. But, again, every battle comes at a price A good General understands the full cost and value of the victory. There is power in the victory, greater than the acquiring plunder. The value is in the testimony!

God has called me to great victory. God has called you to great victory. Not just victory over death for eternal life, victory in your life today!

In *Victorious* you will be given 21 Challenges. The goal of these challenges is not for you just to agree with being victorious; the goal is to equip you with practical changes you can make to live in victory! These challenges are taken from what God has revealed to Siobhan and I about living victoriously in our lives. These keys are not just for conceptual victories, or hypothetical victories, but for real, every day, supernatural life victories. *Victorious* is what truly victorious daily living should look like.

I have been honored to partner with my wife as we have received and walked out these revelations together, encouraged one another, challenged each other, and contended together for victory. Now we get to share these revelations with you and together we all get to live victoriously!

HOW TO USE THIS BOOK

We all have those books that sit lining our shelves for months, maybe years. They taunt us with promised knowledge, wisdom, ideas, and solutions for everything: how to fix our marriage, how to set up a retirement, what could and should happen when Jesus returns (and how you are supposed to feel about it when it happens.) Some are great books, some not so great. In the end, it doesn't really matter because they are just sitting on your shelf doing what even the Classics do over time, collecting dust.

This is not that kind of book.

Well, it shouldn't be. *Victorious* is not designed to sit on a shelf anywhere and collect dust. Instead, it is a practical, easy-to-use (and reuse), down-and-dirty, nitty-gritty kind of book. If you utilize this book the way it is intended, a year from now it will look tattered and worn, dog eared, crinkled, with spine broken, highlighted, underlined, circled and re-circled. It is compact enough to throw in your bag, backpack, or purse and take with you on your best days, worst days, and the days in between. *Victorious* spurs you on to a more abundant life, lifts you up when you are feeling down, and encourages you to take that next step when you don't feel like walking any more.

This is neither a book about perfect people who have it all figured out, or a compilation of great conceptual ideas to fix your life that have no practical application. Rather, it contains accounts of real people who have faced real life and connected with a very real God.

This book is not a race.

Resist the urge to finish this book quickly or hurry to the end so you can start reading the next book in the queue. Take it slow - spend some time reflecting on your responses to the Challenge questions.

From that new understanding, let the book reveal to you greater truth about how God sees you and who He wants to be to you. Grow from there.

This is a "Yes...and" book. As in: "Yes" I will take that cup of coffee, "and" I would like that donut, too. "Yes" I will have a slice of pizza, "and" a side of ranch dressing. "Yes" I will read whatever amazing book may help me with what I am facing right now, "and" I will continue doing the *Victorious* challenges to positively impact and strengthen my life.

Then, once you have fully integrated the *Victorious* challenges, pass it on to a friend. Your side notes, written in the margins, will give your friend greater insight into your battles and your victories. Not only will the book help them in their journey, but the process of you becoming victorious will encourage and spur them on as well!

Victorious is a book of practical insight, supernatural keys, and powerful prayers to help you have... well... a victorious life.

It contains 21 challenges. You may use some as a daily challenge. (We do not recommend taking on more than one challenge per day.) Other challenges you may want to take more time to pursue - days, or weeks. The goal isn't to just get through one challenge and move on to the next. The idea is for each challenge to be transforming. So take *Victorious* one day at a time, or as many days as you need. Read it, respond to it, pray through it, and then live victoriously. Because a victorious life is a powerful life.

CHALLENGE
— 1 —
WINNING MATTERS

- 1 CORINTHIANS 15:57 -

...but thanks be to God, who gives us the victory through our Lord Jesus Christ.
1 Corinthians 15:57

We all have a desire to be victorious, don't we? Victory for you may look very different from another's definition or goal.

Every time you experience victory in your life, that's a *win*.

Victorious living is not about just getting through the day, making it until Friday, or only surviving until your next vacation... or first vacation. It is about overcoming, breaking through, gaining a victory that feels like a *win* to you.

1

What *would* feel like a win today? Specifically, what would a win look like in your current relationships? What about your workplace? Consider your home or your finances. Have you thought about a *win* in your dreams? Write it down, spell it out.

Maybe, for you, it's not the big or final victory, but another mark in the "win" category of your life. Your *win* is determined only by you. So, for you, what would personal victory look like?

Do you ever wake up expecting a participation trophy? "Ok God, I am awake, I am alive, and now I'm getting out of bed. That should count for something!" We have some sad news for you. There are no participation trophies in life. Victorious living often requires a change in thinking, attitude, and expectation. A victorious life is a life of wins.

To be victorious you have to first understand that winning **matters**. Your winning matters to God. That is why He sent Jesus to *win* on your behalf. Jesus conquered sin and death. He did not *win* so that you could just make it through today with only the hope of "one day" experiencing eternal life. No. The price He paid on the cross was to give you life (and life more abundantly) today!

Paul was very clear when he spoke to the church of Corinth. 1 Corinthians 9:24 says, *Do you not know that in a race all the runners run, but only one gets the prize?*

Wait, what?! You might be thinking, "Paul, that is not fair." Our culture says we should all get a prize if we are running. But Paul's challenge is clear, we should run in such a way as to get the prize! In other words, run to **win**.

Here is some good news. You are to run as though to win the prize, but you are not racing against me. And, you are not running against your family or friends. The race isn't with those around you. The goal is for you to win, not over people, but over those things that stop you, hinder you, or hold you back—anger, addiction, bitterness, doubt, depression, lack, or worry.

The even better news is you never have to do it alone. Jesus has already paid for your win. You simply get to choose to partner with His win for your victory.

Winning doesn't happen by accident. It may require a transformation of your mindset(s). To begin with, if you don't care about winning, or don't understand that winning matters (in your life and in those you influence), it will be hard for you to intentionally partner with Jesus' win for victories in your life.

Winning means not losing—not losing the daily battles that Christ has already paid for and given you power and authority over. The reality of your life may look very different from the win you are contending for. Maybe you could fill a book with all the battles you are facing. So first settle within yourself that you want to win. In fact, say out loud, "Today, in my life, I want to win! I want to be victorious! I am going for the win!"

My son downloaded a game on my phone. It is a silly game of world domination in which the objective is to build armies and take over lands. On days when I am bored or need to clear my head, I find myself playing my son's game. To build up points, I have to defeat other lands and win some battles. A lot of the battles I have known I can't win because I really don't understand the game yet. So, to build up points and to build my army, I often first go for some easy victories, some simple battles.

As Christians, we can get discouraged and even stop battling altogether because we try to take on the toughest battle first, rather than building up our faith with simple victories. As you consider today what a *win* would look like, maybe you need to reconsider your strategy. Don't try to tackle the thing that seems to be defeating you every time, sapping your faith, and destroying your resolve.

First, build up your faith. Celebrate the easier victories in your life. An easy win can mean taking five minutes for yourself, or with your family, with God, or taking a walk to clear your head. Sometimes an easy win is making one healthy choice in your life today. There is power in building up your faith.

Jude 1:20 tells us there is power when you build yourself up in your faith and pray in the Holy Spirit. Take time today to build your faith up and pray. Don't let another day go by without living victoriously, without experiencing victory in your life.

Challenge: Earlier you considered what a *win* looked like for you today. Here is an opportunity for you to write down your responses. When you consider a win, how would that look in your:

1. Current relationships?
2. Workplace?
3. Finances?
4. Dreams?

Prayer: "God, today I invite and release the fullness of Your goodness and power into my life. Jesus, I partner with Your victory in my mind, my spirit, my emotions and my outlook. I break off discouragement and doubt. I refuse to partner with fear or worry. I choose to lay hold of the promise that in You I have victory. God, You are my source and my resource. You are my joy and my peace. In You I can do all things. Today the impossible that is before me becomes possible in You. I declare victory in my home, my relationships, my passions and my pursuits. I will not be hindered by any area of lack. I release the fullness of victory in my life today. I choose to have a great day because today was made for me. In Jesus' name, Amen."

VICTORIOUS

CHALLENGE
— 2 —
PRAY LIKE IT MATTERS

- JAMES 5:16 -

The prayer of a righteous person
is powerful and effective.
James 5:16

Not all prayers are considered equal. Have you heard of "Hail Mary" prayers? We have all prayed some version of them at different times in our lives. You know, as in fourth quarter, bottom of the ninth, ball's in your court, down by 2… 4 … 6 (it doesn't matter), you just need a win. So you throw a Hail Mary pass just hoping for a victory. It's the long shot, impossible, improbable prayer you throw hoping for some miracle to happen, for something to work out, for God to come through.

How often do we wait until we are in the worst possible situation to finally cry out to God, as if He hasn't been with us through all the silly decisions and mistakes we have made up until this point?

James 5:16 tells us *the effectual fervent prayer of a righteous man avails much.* The NIV says *the prayer of a righteous person is powerful and effective.*

We want our prayers to be powerful and effective. We want our prayers to avail much. If there are prayers that are powerful and effective (prayers that avail much), that means there are prayers that are not powerful, not so effective, that do not avail much. Hail Mary passes are thrown, and occasionally, some are even caught. But more often than not, they are either missed, or dropped.

In the same way, sometimes those Hail Mary prayers work. When you are down or in impossible situations, pray whatever prayer you can. Our God certainly can work in the impossible. But if you want a **lifestyle** of victorious living, we encourage you to change your prayer life from Hail Mary passes, to *fervent and effectual*.

Note that we did not say *professional*. There is a difference between effectual and professional. If you think prayer must be professional, you may disqualify yourself thinking, "Since I am not trained, equipped, or dedicated enough to pray perfectly, I do not have to do it." Don't disqualify yourself so quickly. In the Gospels, the woman with the issue of blood, written about in Matthew 9, would definitely not be considered professional. But in her effectual pursuit of an encounter with Christ, she received her victory (healing) while many of the *professional* Pharisees and Sadducees missed out on theirs. She was effectual because of her fervent pursuit of victory.

So what is the *effectual, fervent* prayer James is writing about? Fervent: Passion, intensity, relentless, desirous, persistent. This isn't a whim of a prayer, a casual passing-by prayer, or the brief prayer you offer up before a meal. James is talking about an intentional, unrelenting, perhaps even gut-wrenching prayer of power. This prayer of the heart doesn't stop, give in, or quit. It pursues God at all costs. Substituting words may help you better understand: *the effectual relentless prayer avails much,* or *the effectual persistent prayer is powerful.* The prayer that is intense, passionate, relentless, and desirous, is the prayer that doesn't just avail, it avails much! James goes on to write *the effectual, fervent prayer of a **righteous** man avails much.* Or, *the prayer of a righteous man is powerful and effective.*

What is a righteous man? So often we equate righteousness with perfection or an unattainable level of holiness. How do you attain that in a real world where life stuff happens? Sure, righteousness could work for those who can hide in a bubble of prayer all day in some super level of Christianity. But it seems impossible for the everyday Christian who is just trying to make it through life.

Don't count yourself out so quickly. Again, righteousness is not about perfection, or about living some holy, unattainable lifestyle. Instead, righteousness is about being in right relationship with God. Not perfect relationship, right relationship. It's that place where you allow your heart to line up with His heart, your passions to line up with His passions, your desires to align with His desires. It's about being in a right (lined up) relationship. When you align your heart with God's heart, then pursue Him passionately and relentlessly on behalf of the things that are already His heart, your prayer avails much. (It is effective and powerful.)

So what is on God's heart? God cares about His creation, about injustices, the needs of third world countries, and about the dissolute. He also cares about you. YOU are on the heart of God! Your concerns, your battles and your victories matter to God. It is not wrong to pray for you, your life, your family, your needs, and your issues. Jesus died for you. You matter. You matter to Him.

Christ spent everything He had pursuing you and passionately chasing you down to let you know that you are important to Him. Your victory is very important to Him. You are on His heart. Knowing that, you can now pray intensely, passionately, and relentlessly. Pray like it matters. Pray like **you** matter. Seek Him like never before; do not let up, do not give in, do not get discouraged. If you have knocked, knock again. If you have sought, seek again. God does not just want you to have victory over death, He wants you to have victory in life. He longs for you to have victory today!

Challenge: Consider and write down your responses to the following questions:

1. When was the last time you threw up a Hail Mary prayer? How did God answer it?
2. Have you ever disqualified yourself from receiving God's blessings because you weren't *professional* enough in your Christianity?
3. What is God wanting you to understand about righteousness vs. right relationship?

Prayer: "God, today I seek Your face. If there is anything in my life that is holding me back from connecting with You, I am sorry. Please forgive me. I long for my heart to be aligned with Your heart. If there is any area of anger or unforgiveness, forgive me. I want nothing keeping my love back from You and from knowing You more. Today, God, I choose to pursue the fullness of Your promises for my life.

I release healing as my right as a son/daughter of the Most High. I release abundance as a promise from a good God. I release provision as an heir of the King. Stir in me a greater passion and desire for Your promises to be revealed in and through my life. I will not settle for less than the fullness of what You have spoken over me, my relationships, my family, my dreams and my desires. Today I declare victory in my life as I live today victoriously. In Jesus' name, Amen."

VICTORIOUS

CHALLENGE
— 3 —
OLD DOG, NEW TRICKS

- LUKE 11:1 -

One day Jesus was praying in a certain place.
When He finished, one of His disciples said to
Him, "Lord, teach us to pray, just as John
taught his disciples."
Luke 11:1

Wouldn't it be great to already have natural born talent in every area of your life? To know how to do everything you need to do, and do it well? When I was younger, I wanted to play the piano well—to have been just born with a great gift and ability to play flawlessly. That didn't happen. When we realize that skill level takes practice, patience, and work, our response can be, "Fine, I will simply try something else." But even being gifted with natural talent requires more.

My son recently signed up for wrestling. Although he had never wrestled before, he was really good at it. Within his first month of wrestling he moved from JV to Varsity. He began wrestling kids who had been at the sport for years. He had some natural born ability to wrestle, so he won matches. Then he went to a competition where nothing he did worked. He lost match after match. I heard a conversation between Evan and his coach as he was asking what he could do to win. He wanted to know why he was losing. His coach said, "You have reached the point where talent and strength have met with skill and training." He explained that the only thing Evan could do from here was to get better or quit. That was a decisive time for my son and a choice that only he could make. He turned to me and said, "Dad, I guess I only have one option. I have to get better."

When I was first saved I would pray when I had needs. When prayer alone didn't seem to work, I would try something else, like my own ability or power. That often got me into trouble. My heart was right, my passion was there. I just didn't know what I was doing, or how faith worked. So I would quit praying and try something else. Does that sound familiar? How many times in our life do we quit on prayer and try something else? How many times do we quit on prayer and try to fix things in our own power? How many times does that get us into all sorts of trouble: in relationships, in finances, in our home, or at our job? It can bring trouble with a capital "T."

Yes, there is power in that desperate Hail Mary prayer at any time because God hears those prayers, and He cares. In Challenge 2 we also learned that we can be taught to be more effective in our prayer life. The Disciples understood that there was more to prayer than just throwing up a desperate plea to the heavens. Having seen powerful prayers that worked, they understood that there was more to prayer than just words, or going through the motions. So they did one of the most powerful acts found in the Gospels. They asked Jesus to ...*teach us to pray...*

Being taught something new requires learning, skill, practice, trial and error, development and ultimately getting better. In our lives, some of us have been taught bad practices, habits or skills and now we must unlearn those very things. We may need to relearn new, healthier ways to position ourselves for victorious living. For Jesus to teach us anything we must be willing to be taught. Most of us are willing to pray and many have an idea of what prayer looks like, or can look like. But are we willing to be taught? Can old dogs really learn new tricks? Yes, always, if we are willing to say, "Teach me."

Jesus accepts the challenge and His response is revolutionary. In John 11:2, He said to them, *When you pray, say: Father...* The NKJV says *our* Father... This changes everything. That one word, *Father* forever defines His identity and ours. When you pray, who God is to you and who you are to Him matters.

Before we go on or do anything else, let's make absolutely sure you understand this. When you pray, your ability to see God as a good Father, and to see you as His chosen, loved child, matters. The truth of your identity (and restored identity) is huge in God's heart. It has been, since the beginning. Jesus gave everything so we can be restored to our

Father. Why? Our right understanding of the truth of both God's and our identity will transform our prayer life.

In John 11, Jesus was talking to a group of Jewish men, who had once been Jewish boys, and who had Jewish fathers. When Jesus spoke, they knew exactly what He was saying when He used the word *Father*. In the Jewish culture, a father equipped you spiritually, taught you the trade, set the course for your life, and determined your career. A father invited you to partner with him in his business. So when Jesus said *Our Father,* He opened the door to redefine the identity of all those young men. They were now given permission to follow in the trade, to partner in the family business, and to be taught by God, their Father. This was an unheard-of concept. It would mean no need for a Rabbi, no need for a Pharisee, no need for someone to read scripture to them. They were now part of the family.

Understanding God as their Father created an invitation for an intimate relationship with Him. It redefined their identity, just as it also defines ours. If He is our Father, then we are His children, and we are heirs to His inheritance. If God is our Father, then we are sons and daughters of the King; we are royalty. Jesus let them (and us) know that when you pray, remember you are sons and daughters speaking to your Father. As you partner with God; you have authority, right and access to all that He has. He cares for you and you matter deeply to Him. He said all this in one word, *Father*.

Often I have found myself in a room filled with people and much commotion going on around me: talking, laughing, people speaking directly to me, or to others, some asking me questions, and many vying for my attention. In the middle of all that chaos if someone were to ask me for a favor I would probably say "yes." I care about people and try to be a helpful. But given everything else going on in the moment, it is highly possible that later I would forget. However, if, in that same scenario with all that noise and busyness, my wife was to walk into the room and ask me for a favor, not only would I remember I said yes, but I would make sure I did it. I would make that effort because our relationship and intimacy level is deeper; we each know our identity in relation to each other. Why? First, and most importantly, I love her! She is my everything and we have an amazing marriage. Second, it has a great deal to do with who she is, who she is to me and who I am to her. She never has to do anything else, be anything else, earn anything else to get more of me, she has all my attention already.

Now, imagine you have full revelation of your identity to God and His identity to you. You would understand that you are not just a persistent peasant begging the King. You are not one of many vying for His attention. There is nothing more that you have to do or to be. When you call out, "Father," He stops all to focus His undying attention on you. You have full access to Him and He longs for you to succeed, to be victorious. Why? Because He loves you. You are a child of the King. He is your Heavenly Father.

Try it and see. Try changing your view of Him to a loving Father and viewing yourself as a son or daughter of the King and **then** pray. Passionately pursue Him with unrelenting fervor and see what it does to your prayer life—to your victorious life.

Like with many things, some of us will pick this up quicker and others of us it will take time. Some may have damage of years of emotional, physical or spiritual abuse that we have to undo and unlearn. Or, some may carry an identity of what others have spoken over us instead of who God says that we are. We have to learn what it truly means to be a son or a daughter.

This will take practice. And practice comes from doing it over and over and over again.

Remember, prayer is intimate and an intimate prayer is a powerful prayer.

Challenge: Consider, then write down your responses:

1. When was the last time you quit on prayer because your prayers did not seem to be answered? What does God want you to know about those prayers?
2. How are you challenged with understanding God as a *good* Father?

3. What does it mean for you to be a son or daughter of God?

Prayer: "Heavenly Father, You are my Father who loves me unconditionally. Help me to change my view of You, to see You as a loving, caring Father who loves me and wants me to be victorious in every area of my life. Help me to change my view of me, as a son/daughter of the King. Help me to transform my identity and to see myself as You see me through new and renewed eyes. Help me to walk in a right understanding of my identity. Give me the desire and strength to pursue You with confidence and to stand boldly before Your throne. In Jesus' name, Amen."

VICTORIOUS

CHALLENGE
— 4 —

HOW HUNGRY ARE YOU?

- MATTHEW 5:6 -

Blessed are those who hunger and thirst for righteousness for they shall be filled.
Matthew 5:6

How hungry are you? When I was growing up my mom would ask me that question, often before going shopping, or several hours before the next meal. When she asked, I would wonder, "How hungry am I now?" or, "How hungry am I going to be?" Was she asking how hungry I feel or how much food I felt I needed? Were we talking "last meal ever" kind of hunger or "you will eat again"?

I had to consider all these things to determine my hunger level and answer correctly. Otherwise, when dinner time came I might suffer. To be safe, I would always answer the question like any growing boy, "I am very hungry!"

God challenges us with that same question, "How hungry are you?" He is not asking, "How much do you need Me today?" Nor is He asking how hungry are you going to be in the future. The truth is, we all might be willing to be hungry for a move of God when we are in a tight spot or when we need a miracle. But how hungry are we *daily* for God? It is important to know that answer for yourself. Your God hunger is a key to victory and to living a life that is victorious.

Blessed are those who hunger and thirst for righteousness for they shall be filled.

Do you see what God is showing us here? To be hungry in some Christian circles implies you did something wrong to be hungry, or God did something wrong not to fill you. Neither of these are correct, but such assumptions can keep us resistant to hungering for a right relationship with God. Where the world considers hunger a negative, God calls you blessed when you are hungry. God takes a perceived negative and turns it into a positive. In His kingdom being hungry gives you an opportunity to be filled.

Growing up I had a friend who, unlike me, had a very high metabolism. He was super skinny, but always hungry and always eating. He could eat all the things that I was never allowed to eat. We would finish a full lunch and he would still be hungry for more. At the time I wished I could be him. His hunger was awesome!

In this verse in Matthew, God promises the hungry *shall* be filled. I love the word *shall*. (I would highlight and underline that word.) Other versions say *will*. They *will* be filled. God doesn't say can be, may be, could be, or might be filled. He says *will* be filled. In Matthew 7, Jesus goes on to say *seek and you will find*. He is giving a heavenly guarantee that if you hunger, if you seek, if you pursue, you will be filled, you will find, and you will encounter.

In God's Kingdom, passion places a demand on the heavens that must be fulfilled. When you hunger, you draw on the heavens and create a pull so powerful that it draws down the heavens and meets you right where you are. Perfection does not do this, holiness does not do this; but hunger does, desire does, and passion does.

Being hungry does not require you to come before the king as a pauper begging for scraps. Hunger should stir within us a desire for God and for more than yesterday's encounter. We want today's encounter to be one where we experience God in a way that is fresh, new, and alive. Hunger for God causes you to not only want the fullness of everything that God has promised, but to be unwilling to be satisfied with anything less than all that God has promised for your life. It raises your expectations to supernatural levels because you walk in the assurance that your God is supernatural.

Today, God is asking, "How hungry are you?" Not, "How hungry are you going to be?" or, "How hungry do you want to be?" Instead He asks, "How hungry are you for Me?" Maybe you have been on a Slim Fast Diet of encounters with God, or living off past encounters or experiences instead of current ones. Maybe you even believed you are doing God a favor, by not asking for more.

If that is you, please know God is big enough to bless you outrageously yesterday, today **and** tomorrow. Take a moment now and write down the areas of your life where you have not been hungry, or have not invited God in. Where do you want, or need more hunger for a deeper relationship with God? Where do you need a miracle? Start there. It's time to get hungry.

What if you don't feel hungry, but you want to? Sometimes you don't know how hungry you are until you start eating. This is one of those places were daily prayer and encountering God helps. Start today to taste and see that the Lord is good. Then taste again, and again. Once you have had that encounter with God, say, "That was good, God. Now I want some more."

You will be blessed. You will be filled. You will be Victorious.

Challenge: Consider, and write down your response to the following:

1. In what area(s) do you already feel satisfied with your relationship with God?

2. In what ways do you believe God is calling you to be more hungry for a deeper relationship with Him?

3. In what way(s) would you like to experience God as you never have before?

Prayer: "God, stir within me today a hunger for more of You. Increase my desire for the fullness and abundance of all You have for me. Don't let me be satisfied with my God encounters from yesterday. My heart cries out to know You and Your goodness in ways that enable me to see myself as You see me. Make me brave. I hunger for Your supernatural presence to be manifested in my life. Allow the desires of my heart to place a demand on the heavens that must be met. Meet me here, today, in my life, in my pursuits, in my desires. I long for You to bless and fill my relationships, my home, my work, my family, my church, and my life. Today I refuse to settle for less than all You have for me. I know that only You can satisfy the hunger within me and make me victorious. In Jesus' name, Amen."

CHALLENGE
— 5 —

DON'T SETTLE FOR THE MIRACLE WHEN YOU HAVE A PROMISE

- 1 KINGS 18:41 -

*And Elijah said to Ahab, "Go, eat and drink,
for there is the sound of a heavy rain."*
1 Kings 18:41

One of my favorite sections of scripture has always been in 1 Kings when Elijah calls down fire from Heaven to consume the sacrifice before the Lord.

This miracle happens via an epic showdown between the prophets of Baal and Elijah, the Prophet of God. There is name calling, challenging, peacocking, and gloating. It's awesome. And, at the end of it all, God wins.

When the Prophets of Baal fail because their gods do nothing and their sacrifice is not consumed, Elijah ups the ante. He has water poured on his altar three times, saturating the sacrifice, the altar, and making an impossible situation even more impossible. Then God sent fire down to consume the sacrifice... and the altar... and every drop of water. It was a miracle!

However, that wasn't enough for Elijah: God had promised rain. So, instead of celebrating, holding a revival service, or a worship service, he goes to the top of Mount Carmel and begins to pray for rain. He doesn't just pray for rain, he contends for it (even though they were in the middle of a drought).

Elijah didn't relent, give in, or quit. Despite the fact his servant reported there was not even a cloud in the sky. Circumstances did not line up, but Elijah's faith was not dependent upon the facts. The miracle (fire) built his faith to contend for the promise (rain). The fire was good, but the rain was better. The fire fell in a concise locale, but the rain saturated the land.

Sometimes we mistake the *power* of God for the *promise* of God in our life. His demonstration of power is to build up your faith so you can boldly step forward and lay hold of your promise.

Laying hold of your promise will require more of you, and ask you to risk in ways you have never risked before.

Watching God showcase His power is easy. Risking big by boldly stepping out in faith to lay hold of a destiny that is beyond your ability is not easy. By the time God asks that of you, He will have built your faith to do it.

Consider the Israelites. While they were out in the wilderness, they were a walking testimony to the power of God. They wondered the wilderness for 40 years. Each day they would wake up and see Manna (dried bread) on the ground, provided for them by God. It was a miracle. When they were thirsty, God provided water from a rock. He protected them while in the wilderness and gave them direction as well; a cloud by day and fire by night.

Definitely awesome, amazing, great, and totally God... but it was not the promise. They were settling for bread and water; their promise was a land flowing with milk and honey.

Let this sink in. The Israelites celebrated a miracle that was less than their promise. It was God providing for their daily needs so one day they would realize that He had created them for more.

Now, replace Israelites with your name. How many times have you settled for less than what God has called you to? How many times have you settled for a miracle in place of the promise that God has spoken over your life, your relationships, your family, your passions and dreams? How many times have you settled for the fire, because, let's admit it, fire is cool. The fire is the "Wow!" But the fire was never meant to be the end all. The miracle is to encourage you, challenge you, and call you upward toward the full promises of God over your life.

Here is a challenge. First, consider the miracles in your life. Think about the past five years. When have you felt, experienced, or seen any miracle (fire) of God? Write them down. If you can't think of any, ask God to show you where He has done the miraculous on your behalf. Write those down.

Your list may include circumstances that should have ended badly, but didn't, or opportunities that miraculously came your way. Remember, any time you have had a miraculous "Wow!" moment. You are now positioned to contend for your promise.

It is important that you know the difference between the promise and the miracle in your life. Now, take time today and write down some of the promises that God has spoken over you that have yet to take place. List the promises over your relationships, your family, your health or wholeness, and promises over your dreams and destiny. Write them down and then begin to contend for them. Despite what you see, despite what you feel, despite your circumstances, begin to lay them before your Heavenly Father and contend for their victory. Remember, fire is to ignite your faith, but the rain is a testimony to the whole land.

When the fire fell, nothing changed in the weather for Elijah, and nothing changed in the atmosphere. He didn't feel a rain drop or even moisture. When the fire fell, the only thing that changed was Elijah. His expectations went to supernatural levels and he didn't relent. He prayed. When nothing changed, he kept praying. When his circumstances didn't change, he prayed more. He prayed past the miracle, until the promise came and rain fell and soaked the land.

Challenge: Take time to consider the difference between God's miracles and promises in your life. Write your responses to the following:

1. What miracles has God shown you that He has done on your behalf?
2. What is the greatest promise you are contending for in your life now?
3. Are there any areas where you have settled for a miracle instead of the promise?

Prayer: "Heavenly Father, today in my life I ask for Your fire to fall on me, in me, and ignite my faith to new levels. Stir in me the supernatural belief and certainty that through You all things are possible. Raise my expectations to see, through renewed eyes, supernatural possibilities in my life. Today, I contend for the promises that You have spoken over me, my family, my relationships, my dreams and my destiny. I believe Your Word is true and will not return void. Fill up the areas of my life that feel empty or lacking faith. Allow my fulfilled promise to be a testimony of Your greatness to the world around me. Let Your glory saturate the whole land that they will know the immeasurable love of my God. In Jesus' name, Amen."

VICTORIOUS

CHALLENGE
— 6 —
WHOSE LIGHT IS SHINING?

- MATTHEW 5:14-16 -

You are the light of the world. A town built on a hill cannot be hidden. Neither do people light a lamp and put it under a bowl. Instead they put it on its stand, and it gives light to everyone in the house. In the same way, let your light shine before others, that they may see your good deeds and glorify your Father in Heaven.
Matthew 5:14-16

Have you ever read a scripture verse so many times that it actually shocks you to realize that you have read it wrong for many years? I am not talking about just going back to the Greek and the Hebrew definitions, or exegeting the scripture to find the hermeneutical, or contextual understanding of the author's original intent. Instead, I am talking about a scripture that is right there in plain English, extremely simple, preached about, written about, emblazed on t-shirts, embossed on coffee cups, and you still got it wrong. This is me and about every other person I know who has ever read the scripture.

In the past I have understood the above scripture to say: God is the light, so let your (His) light shine so that people can see God's light through you. The scripture actually says that "you" are the light. Wait a second, Jesus is the light. Didn't Jesus say that He was the way, the truth and the light? Yes, it is true. Jesus is the light. As a believer, with Christ in you, His light is within you. But He also calls **you** the light. Therefore, you can let **your** light shine that people can see *your* good deeds and glorify your Father in Heaven. What does that exactly mean?

For so long I was trying to let my light shine so I could point people to God (the big light up in the sky) shining bright like the sun. After all, He is the light, right? Imagine for a minute taking a flashlight (your light) out of your cupboard, walking outside in the middle of the day, and trying to use the flashlight to direct people's attention towards the sun (His light). To think people would gather around this "phenomenal" event would be ridiculous. Any flashlight pales in comparison to the sun. In fact, no one would even see the flashlight because they would be blinded by the light of the sun if they looked toward it. Yet, this is what we have done for years in Christianity. Many have stood in the full blinding rays of Jesus and tried desperately to point people in His direction. Of course they saw Him; He is an amazing, brilliant light! Then we congratulate ourselves on shining so well. Truth is, you will never really know for sure if you are shining unless you stand in darkness.

For years I never knew if my Christian flashlight worked because I was always standing in the middle Christianity where the brilliant rays of Jesus were always shining. Any time I was challenged with darkness, I would blame the darkness for being dark and hide in the "safety" of the light of Christ. That wasn't the challenge Jesus gave His disciples and that is not the challenge He gives you and me.

Jesus said you are the light! Let your light so shine that men would see your good deeds and glorify Him. We are supposed to go into dark places where the light of God is not shining, and we are supposed to shine. How? With sermons? With tracts? With preaching, converting and repeat-after-me prayers? NO! He says let your light so shine that men would see your good deeds. Light shining is good deeds.

God began to challenge me, "What are your good deeds today? How are you going to shine today?" Darkness doesn't mean evil; darkness is anywhere that the Kingdom of God is not established. Where there is fear, shine love. Where there is doubt, shine hope. Where there is sickness, reveal healing. Where there is loneliness, be a friend.

It seems much easier to take our Jesus flashlight and point people to Him. "Do you need a friend? Jesus can be your friend. I am not going to be your friend; I don't even know you. But follow the flashlight and see Jesus right there big and bright and shining." Or, "Do you need love? Don't look at me, I don't even like you. But follow the flashlight to Jesus shining big and bright in the sky somewhere. He will love you." That was never the challenge.

Jesus doesn't need us to point people to Him. He challenges us to reveal Jesus to them, through us, through our good deeds. Then they will glorify our Heavenly Father. Do you want to be victorious in your life, in your pursuits today? Stop pointing people to Jesus and start revealing Jesus, through you... and your good deeds. Remember, you are the light people are going to see, the light that they are going to experience. You are the light of the world, so let your light so shine. Don't just shine a little, don't just kinda shine; **so** shine.

When my wife asks me how she looks in the morning, I can say that she looks beautiful or I can say she looks **so** beautiful! There is power in *so*. Jesus is letting you know that your shine can be *so* bright, at such an extreme level, that when people see you living boldly, loudly, victoriously, they will see Him through you. Don't just shine today, *so* shine!

Take a moment and ask God to show you the things in you that shine brightly to those around you. Write them down. Then ask Him what He has placed in you that you have not yet been able to release or develop to shine. Where does He want you to shine hope, peace, love or joy? Where are you not seeing the opportunities to shine to those around you? Invite Him to open your eyes. Then, when He does, say "Yes!" to what He is showing you.

Challenge: Consider, then write down your responses:

1. In what ways has it been difficult to see yourself as the light?
2. Where is God inviting you to shine brighter with what He has placed in you?
3. What would **so** shining look like in your life?

Prayer: "Heavenly Father, let me **so** shine today that my life is a testimony to the greatness of You, a great God! In all that I do, everywhere I go, in all that I place my hand to, let my good deeds bring glory to You. Give me opportunities today to reveal Your love to those who are hurting, reveal hope to those who feel hopeless, reveal Your healing today to those who are broken, and reveal Your goodness today to those who are searching. Today, Lord, I declare and receive Your glory in my life, my relationships, my family and my destiny. Fill me with strength, boldness and bravery to shine brightly to those around me so they will glorify You. In Jesus' name, Amen."

VICTORIOUS

CHALLENGE
— 7 —

GOD BLESS YOU

- 1 CHRONICLES 4:10 -

*Jabez cried out to the God of Israel, "Oh, that
You would bless me and enlarge my territory!
Let Your hand be with me, and keep me from
harm so that I will be free from pain."
And God granted his request.*
1 Chronicles 4:10

I was sitting at the Department of Motor Vehicles
for the glorious experience of renewing my Driver's
License, when a little boy and his mother sat down
next to me. The little boy, about 6 years old,
sneezed. I turned to him and said, "God bless you."
Then he sneezed again. "God bless you," I repeated.
Then he sneezed again. "God bless you," I said
again. I saw him gearing up for another good
sneeze when his mother tapped him on the shoulder
and said, "Don't be selfish." The little boy looked

49

at me, with a cheeky smile, then let out one more sneeze. "God bless you!"

I have remembered his mother's words, probably better than he has. "Don't be selfish." She implied, "You had one blessing, two blessings, three… that is enough now." It wasn't enough, not for the little boy—he wanted just one more. In fact, I think if he thought he could have gotten 5 or 6 more blessings he would have gone for it.

"Don't be selfish" is how the enemy has tricked many of us into not receiving many of our blessings. It seems blessings (or wanting blessings) has become a bad word in the Christian culture. It can be considered selfish, vain, or singular. Yet in 1 Chronicles, Jabez cries out to God. He even uses an exclamation point for emphasis. He says, *Oh that You would bless me and enlarge my territory!* Then it says that God granted Jabez his request. God does not say, "Jabez, don't be selfish." Instead, it seems He says, "Yes! You figured it out, you got it!"

It is important to understand that we have a God who loves to bless us. He longs to pour out His goodness over and into our lives. This revelation is vital to the pursuit of blessings. In Matthew 7 God tells us that if we, being imperfect parents, know how to give good gifts to our children, how much more will our Heavenly Father give good gifts to those who ask Him. Because of what He said, pursuing and receiving blessings as singular and selfish couldn't be further from the truth.

Two things happen with blessings. First, God longs to bless you because your life is a testimony to the greatness of a great God! In our last challenge we explained how He longs to pour out, in and through you because you are the light of the world. For some reason in Christian circles we have said, "You have eternal life. Stop there, be happy with that, and don't be selfish." God says He came to give you life and life more abundantly. He wants you to have more, not just enough. He wants to bless you abundantly because you are the Jesus that people are going to see; your life is the victory of His victory! That matters. Second, your blessing was never meant to stop with you. God wants to bless you so that you can bless those around you. Blessings should not stop, but flow, in and through you. You are designed to be a conduit for the goodness of

God, and have that goodness revealed through you. Blessings only become singular when we stop sharing them, when we stop shining.

Jabez had such a powerful understanding of God's blessings that He was unwilling to live life without them. He knew they were his right, so he contended for them. Talk about a powerful prayer! When flying on an airline, during part of the pre-flight checklist the flight attendant will explain that in the event of low air pressure in the cabin, oxygen masks will fall. They then instruct passengers to place them firmly over their head and breathe. If you are traveling with someone who needs assistance, they emphasize the importance of you placing your mask on first, before trying to help someone else. Why? You will be of little help to anyone else if you become oxygen deprived and go unconscious. The point is, to be effective, you must first get yours so that you can then help those around you. God is in Heaven wanting you to get your blessings so you can then bless those around you. If you are not seeing it yet, contend for it.

In Genesis, Jacob contends with God for his blessing. He actually wrestles with God and says, *I will not let go until You bless me.* When is the last time you actually contended with God over your blessing? Most of us would be very hesitant (maybe shocked) to pray the prayer, "Lord bless me!" And even less inclined to contend with God for that blessing.

The dreams, pursuits and influence that God has called you to, you cannot do without His blessings in your life. How many times have you attempted to pursue a dream without His blessings, feeling that to ask for more would be selfish? God is reminding you that His blessings are for you, for your victory, and for your testimony. They bring Him glory.

Your challenge is to write down any blessings you have been hesitant, unwilling or afraid to ask God for. In what areas of your life would you like the blessings of God? In what ways do you want Him to bless you? What would enlarging your territory look like? Where are you asking Him to make His presence known and show that His hand is with you? What pain or harm do you want God to keep you from? In what ways would you like to bless others? Ask God to bless you. Pray, contend and go for it! Don't let go till you get it!

Challenge: Consider, then write down your responses:

1. Have you ever felt that wanting God to bless you more is selfish?
2. Where are you asking God to enlarge your territory?
3. In what ways would you like to be blessed so you could then share those blessings with others? What are you asking for?

Prayer: "Lord, bless me and enlarge my territory! Let Your hand be with me and keep me from harm so that I will be free from pain. Let my life be a testimony to Your greatness. Bless me outrageously so I can bless those around me and reveal the love of a good God. Equip me today with everything I need to be successful and victorious in the things You have called me to do. Place in me a longing, a hunger, a desire for the fullness of all You have for me. Give me spiritual strength and boldness to contend and not relent until I have seen these blessings manifested in my life! Today, God, I give You glory in all I do. In Jesus' name, Amen."

CHALLENGE
— 8 —
LISTEN

- DANIEL 9:19 -

Lord, listen! Lord, forgive! Lord, hear and act! For Your sake, my God, do not delay, because your city and your people bear Your Name.
Daniel 9:19

Have you ever heard someone pray, "God, if it is Your will…"? You may have even prayed the same way before. Perhaps you were in a tough predicament, facing an impossible situation, or your back was against the wall, so you prayed, "Lord, if it is Your will..." Maybe you prayed, "If it is Your will, save me…", "If it is Your will, free me", or "If it is Your will, heal me."

I was in a prayer meeting where a little girl came up for healing. The man praying for her said, "God, if it is Your will, heal this little girl." I was outraged. If it is His will? What does that say to this little girl standing there, "If you don't get healed, it must not have been God's will." NO! We already know His will! By Christ's stripes we are healed. It is not just His will, it is also our right as sons and daughters of the King!

How often do we trade away that right by instead praying pretentious prayers that have no power? Are we afraid of offending God, or that our confidence will come off as arrogance and God will smite us for our pride?

Hebrews tells us to come in confidence before His throne, to come boldly, confidently before God. There is power in confidence. The enemy has tricked us for so long that we have bought into the idea that God likes self-depreciation more than the confidence He calls us to. Buying into this unintended level of humility can keep you from ever laying hold of the rights and miracles Jesus died for.

God is more offended by tepid prayers than He is of over-confident prayers. An illustration of this is found with Daniel in Daniel 9. He is in a tough spot, again. King Darius is ruling over the Persian Empire. He is the son of one of the most ruthless kings of all time, King Xerxes. So, Daniel begins to pray. Actually, it says that he pleaded with God. There is something powerful about transparent, passionate prayer that does not relent. Daniel ends his prayer in historic fashion, *Lord Listen!* Complete with exclamation point. He is pleading with God to listen, to hear what he is saying. A few verses before this he actually asks God to open His ears and hear and open His eyes and see. Talk about confidence and boldness! Daniel then takes it a step further and tells God to not only listen, but to hear and to act. Daniel challenges God to hear him because he knows there is a difference between hearing and listening. In fact, he tells God that he doesn't want God to simply hear him, Daniel wants God to understand what he is saying and move on his behalf. That is a bold, passionate, powerful prayer.

What would happen if you began to shift your prayer life to pray with this kind of power, passion, and transparency? What would happen if you prayed with this kind of confidence and boldness before the throne of God? Take a moment and consider, in your life today, where do you need God to hear you; to understand you and move on your behalf? Where do you need God to listen, to open His ears and hear and open His eyes and see? What would "open ears" and "eyes on your behalf" look like? Write down your answers.

Daniel then says, do not delay, act quickly, because your people bear your name. He is telling God that it is not enough for God to hear him, it is not enough for God to move, but he needs God to move quickly!

He takes His boldness to another level. Why? Daniel had a full revelation and understood that the people of God were a testimony to God. He knew that God's people were (still are) the light of the world. He challenged God on God's behalf. It was as if he said, "Move and act... for You!" You can pray that in your life too, "God, my life is a testimony to You, so listen! Hear me. Understand me. I need You to move and act with healing. I need You to move and act with provision. I need You to move and act with restoration... not for me but for You! My life is a testimony to the world of the greatness of a great God!"

What would happen if you prayed that way? I can tell you what happened with Daniel. In Daniel 9:23 a prophet comes to Daniel and said, *"As soon as you began to pray a word went out!"*

As soon as you begin to contend for your promise, for the fulfillment of God's best in your life, or for your destiny, something begins to happen! Why? Praying is powerful. It changes the atmosphere and has the power to transform.

Today I want to challenge you to challenge God in your life for the promises that He has spoken over you.

Challenge: Consider, then write down your responses:

1. Have you prayed "If it is God's will" prayers? Has this challenge encouraged you to pray differently?
2. In what ways do you desire to have more confidence when you come before God?
3. In what areas are you contending for God to move on your behalf?

Prayer: "God, listen! Hear my heart cry today, be attentive to my words. I cry out to You, God, to understand and act on my behalf. Where I need healing, heal. Where I need breakthrough, make a way. Where I need victory, give me this day. I am a child of the Most-High God; I bear Your name. Allow my testimony and my life to bring glory to You. Right now, God, even as I pray, I am believing that You are working miracles on my behalf and that You are doing the impossible. I know God that You are a good God and that You love me. I am asking You to... (read the list from your challenge). Today I say thank You that Your mercy and grace are sufficient for me, they are never ending. Today, Lord, I release the victory of Heaven in my life! In Jesus' name, Amen."

CHALLENGE
— 9 —
REMEMBER ME

- JUDGES 16:28 -

O Lord God, please remember me
and please strengthen me...
Judges 16:28

If the enemy can take you out of the battle you will never have a chance to win. You can feel strong and victorious in certain areas of your life, and, at the same time, have soft, squishy places where you feel you don't measure up. Everyone has those areas. Everyone has at least one area that they struggle in: self-control, forgiveness, patience, follow through, faith for healing, belief for finances, the ability to trust and risk big, transparency in love and relationships, or maybe honesty or the ability to keep their word. If the list continued you would find some area where you would agree, "Yes, I struggle there."

That being said, is it really a struggle, or is it a willful defeat? Is it possible you have you given up on yourself or walked away from a growth opportunity in that area? God hasn't given up on you or your growth. A victorious life is one in which every aspect of your life brings glory to God. But the devil is tricky. He will try to get you to disqualify yourself from competing or trying. He wants you to quit the game. Why? How?

We have all failed before, so most of us believe that we will fail again, and again. This can be especially true in any area you may already feel you don't measure up or can't make the cut. We know that God is a God of grace and mercy, so we apply that mercy and grace to our failure. We drop out and move on. This isn't about pointing out sin or any failure of mercy and grace. Rather, it is about the importance of pressing on to victory.

God wants us to win because winning matters. He has already conquered fear, death, poverty, loneliness, depression, addiction... the list is long. He didn't conquer these things for you to continue to be defeated by them daily. He conquered sin and death so that you could have victory. The enemy uses shame to keep us so bound we can shrink back from ever even entering the race. He uses guilt and regret to hold us back from our destiny of living a life that is truly victorious.

I love the prayer that Sampson prays in Judges. Sampson was the leader of the Israelites, who was blessed by God with amazing strength. That same Sampson, turned his back on the covenant promise he made to God over a girl named Delilah and lost it all... including his eyes. Talk about messing up big time.

The world is quick to disqualify. They will say you are not talented enough, qualified enough, or gifted enough. Maybe you have tried and failed like Sampson. But Sampson goes after it one more time. In Judges 16:28 he prays, *O Lord God, please remember me and please strengthen me...* It is such a simple but powerful prayer. Sampson may have messed up, but he did not give up.

God did remember Sampson: his strength came back, and he saved God's people one more time. The enemy counted him out, and he would have been by many religious standards, and by some personal standards. That was what the enemy was hoping for—defeat.

We, too, have the ability to cry out to God in the midst of our toughest time in our hardest areas. Like Sampson, we can say, "God, remember me. Remember the heart that loves You, the heart that pursues You, the heart that tries to get it right and messes up all the time. Remember me, the one that You love, that You pursued, that You gave it all for. Remember me, today, because I need You, God, now more than ever."

Sampson asks God to give him strength. It is a humble prayer that holds power because it is an admittance that he cannot do it without God. It is the knowing that "I don't have the power, the ability, or resource to do it on my own. I need You real in my life."

That request is for partnership with God. That is what God wants more than anything. It is there that God receives the little that we have and partners it with His everything. Our little always becomes powerful in His hands. That is life changing.

Being willing to say, "God, give me strength" is not just about Him making you stronger. It is about Him partnering with who you are. When you feel defeated, it may not be easy to pray, "God, remember me and give me strength." But when you do, God comes in a major way and you begin to walk in powerful victory. Just because the devil has you down does not mean that God counts you out.

Think of the areas in your life where you have been counted out, or looked or felt defeated. Commit them to God, then begin to cry for God to remember you and strengthen you.

Expect and anticipate His answer. He will strengthen you. God longs for you to be victorious in all areas of your life!

Challenge: Consider, then write down your responses:

1. What is an area that you need God to remember you in and give you strength?

2. Where has guilt or regret held you back from living victoriously? It's time to give it to God.

3. In what areas of your life is God wanting to partner with you?

Prayer: "Lord, remember me and strengthen me. Don't let me quit or become satisfied or stagnant in the areas that You have called me to grow. Challenge me to press on to live a victorious life. Strengthen and equip me in every area of my life: spiritual, emotional and physical. I ask You to partner with me in my pursuit of my dreams and destiny and strengthen me in the areas where I am weak. Be my sufficiency and my resource where I lack. Forgive me today for the times I have struggled, failed or quit. Help my life to be a testimony to Your greatness. Reveal that greatness in and through me today. Lord, give me victory this day as I live victoriously in You! In Jesus' name, Amen."

CHALLENGE
— 10 —

POWER MUST LOOK POWERFUL

- ACTS 4:31 -

After they prayed, the place where they were meeting was shaken. And they were all filled with the Holy Spirit and spoke the word of God boldly.
Acts 4:31

I once talked to a friend who said he didn't believe in God. I asked him why? What kept him away? He answered, "Christians say one thing and live another." I asked, "Like being a hypocrite, condemning sin but then living in it?" "Not really." He explained that they say they have a God of power, but have never seen power. Christians say they have a God of healing, but have not seen anyone healed. They say they have a God of joy, peace, and love, but he can't see joy in their lives. They seem to be just as stressed out as everyone else. He told me, "Power must look powerful, or what's the point?"

Here's the truth: Power must look powerful and victory must look victorious.

I want to see the power of God in my life. I don't want to just talk about power, I want to **live** powerfully. I don't want to just talk about victory, I want to live victoriously.

In the book of Acts, we see powerful results of prayer. *After they prayed the place where they were meeting was shaken.* Their prayer was so powerful that once they finished praying the whole place was physically shaken. Now that is a powerful testimony to those around them. They moved from just talking the talk to experiencing the real deal.

Reading a scripture like this, where the power of God was revealed in such a dynamic way, makes you want to know what kind of prayer they prayed. Acts 4:23-31 helps us discover the power of their prayer:

On their release, Peter and John went back to their own people and reported all that the chief priests and the elders had said to them. When they heard this, they raised their voices together in prayer to God. "Sovereign Lord," they said, "You made the heavens and the earth and the sea, and everything in them. You spoke by the Holy Spirit through the mouth of your servant, our father David:

"Why do the nations rage and the peoples plot in vain? The kings of the earth rise up and the rulers band together against the Lord and against his anointed one.

Indeed, Herod and Pontius Pilate met together with the Gentiles and the people of Israel in this city to conspire against Your Holy Servant Jesus, whom you anointed. They did what Your power and will had decided beforehand should happen. Now, Lord, consider their threats and enable Your servants to speak Your word with great boldness. Stretch out Your hand to heal and perform signs and wonders through the name of Your Holy Servant Jesus. After they prayed, the place where they were meeting was shaken. And they were all filled with the Holy Spirit and spoke the Word of God boldly.

69

Let's look at four keys to their victory through prayer:

Key #1: Verse 4:23-24: *On their release, Peter and John went back to their own people and reported all that the chief priests and the elders had said to them... they raised their voices together in prayer...* **There is power in community!**

Despite what the enemy says, despite what you may think, despite how being around other people makes you feel, there is strength in community. God designed it that way. You and I together will always be more powerful than you or me on our own. There is a reason why in times of struggle we want to run away and hide. Or, when we fail or face tough situations, we try to get through it on our own. The enemy knows that we are weaker on our own.

It happened with Adam and Eve all the way back in the Garden of Eden. They sinned, then hid in shame. We do the same thing today. The enemy uses shame to get us to isolate, then we try to tackle the toughest stuff on our own. God gave us family and community so we can join together, be strengthened, and live victoriously.

Peter and John knew this. So instead of hanging their head in shame, embarrassed that they got caught and locked up, they pressed into community. They did the opposite of what the enemy wanted them to do.

Every time you choose to do the opposite of what the enemy wants, you are taking the right steps toward victory.

The first part of this challenge is to list your community. Who are your close friends, the prayer warriors you know that you can go to, the person whose advice you trust, or you can tell everything to, and your accountability partner(s)? Look at the list. If your list is full, you probably already understand the importance of community. Thank God for them and continue to build your *power* team. If your list is short (or blank), today can be a life changer for you! List those you know that could pour into different areas of your life. Today, choose to develop community.

Key #2: Verse 24 continues: *Sovereign Lord, they said, You made the heavens and the earth and the sea, and everything in them.* **Remind God of who He is!**

You see many accounts in scripture of people praying and reminding God of His great deeds, awesome might, and His great power. They declare to Him how He set them free, performed miracles, provided, or made a way. They recount to Him His wonder and His might. Why would they do this? Well, you can be sure they were not doing it for His benefit. He knows how awesome He is; He is God. He is aware of the miracles He has performed; He was there.

These prayers were not for His benefit, but for theirs. They were building up their faith. They were encouraging themselves in the spirit by reminding themselves that they are partnered with the great and mighty God; the God who sets captives free; the God who made the heavens and the earth and everything around them; the God who heals, provides, and makes a way when there seems to be no way. When you start declaring these things, proclaiming the Word of God, it builds your faith to supernatural levels.

Peter and John ran to their community and started testifying about how great God is and what He had done. Just a short time before Peter and John were in prison where everything seemed impossible, all hope was lost. Now they start to feel a shaking happening, first in them.

When your heart gets stirred, your faith will rise. Begin to remind yourself of the power of God in your life. Take inventory of times when you know God has done powerful things in your life, and in those around you. Say them out loud and build up your faith.

Key #3: In verse 29 they prayed: *Now, Lord, consider their threats...* **Give threats made against you to God!**

Peter and John had very real threats made against their lives. While you may not have physical threats against you, you have spiritual threats made by the enemy against you every day. Threats are made against your relationships, your marriage, your children, your finances, your reputation, and against your personal success. Many of us tend to just "deal" with them, or worse, just "live" with them rather than lift them up to God. We accept that threats will be there, there is not much we can do, so there is no use complaining about them.

Have you ever wondered why some people may have victory in finances while you do not, or others experience victory in health, but you don't? Maybe they decided they were not going to just "deal with it" any more. Maybe they decided to hand these threats to God.

Peter and John knew their life was a testimony to the greatness of a great God. They were not going to allow any threats of the enemy to remain.

You don't have to either. Take the challenge and write down threats that the enemy has made against you, your family or your destiny that you have allowed to remain. Now, submit them to God and let them go.

Key #4: Verse 30: *Stretch out Your hand to heal and perform signs and wonders through the name of your Holy Servant Jesus.* **Move in power!**

Power must be powerful. It is not just enough to just talk about power, signs and wonders, or about healing. We need to seek it out. One of my professors in Bible College would say, "A move of God is not when you say that God is moving, but when others stand back and say, 'God must be moving.'" Power is not when you say you are powerful, but when others step back and say, "That is powerful!"

Peter and John knew this. They pressed into community where they could be encouraged, challenged, stretched, and strengthened. They began to testify to one another, building up their faith, reminding themselves of what God had done. They chose not to entertain threats; they submitted them to God. But it doesn't stop there. They told God they want to see power, real tangible power in their life. How is that powered realized? It is demonstrated through signs and wonders, healing and miracles. You can pray the same prayer today.

Your challenge: Stir up in you the power of a great God. Tell God you want Him to stretch out His hand to show you healing and perform signs and miracles! Don't go another day without seeing His power manifest in a real way.

After they prayed, the place where they were meeting was shaken. It was then that the power was powerful.

Challenge: Today you have one challenge for each of the four Keys. Take as much time as you need to respond:

1. What did the list of your community show you about your sense of community?
2. What area in your life is God reminding you that He is God and He has done great things?
3. What spiritual threats made against you and those you love do you need to hand over to God today?
4. What signs, wonders and miracles are you contending to see and experience?

Prayer: "Today, God, I glorify You, the creator of the heavens and the earth. I praise Your name for what You have done in my life. You have pursued me, restored me, renewed me and redeemed me. I thank You for the breakthrough You have done in my life. Today, God, I submit to You every threat made against me, my life, my family, my identity, my destiny, or my relationships. The threat of fear must go in Jesus' name. The threat of poverty must leave. The threat of doubt, worry, or depression, has no place in my life or in the lives of those around me. Today, God, I long to see Your power manifested in my life with signs, wonders, and healings. Give me an opportunity today to showcase Your power to those around me. Allow my life to be a testimony to the greatness of You, a great God. Allow me to live in victory and power today as I declare that in You I am victorious. In Jesus' name, Amen."

VICTORIOUS

CHALLENGE
— 11 —

THE POWER OF CONFIDENCE

- PHILLIPIANS 1:6 -

Being confident of this, that He who began
a good work in you will carry it on to
completion until the day of Christ Jesus.
Philippians 1:6

I once gathered a group of people together and asked them to answer questions about confidence.

My first question was, "If you were at your workplace and someone walked in with an extreme level of confidence, what would they look like? Describe them." The answers started with the external attributes, such as, how nicely they dressed, how they presented themselves, how put together they looked, and how they invested in their presentation.

Descriptions moved on to character traits: a successful person would be a risk taker, one who spoke with power and lived boldly. In the workplace, that was their definition of a confident person.

I then asked them the same question, with a small change. "If someone were to walk into the church today with an extreme level of confidence, what would they look like?" Instantly comments began to fly describing the person as cocky, arrogant, conceited, proud, and haughty. Wow! In the world confidence looks like power and in the church confidence looks like arrogance?

We are called to influence the world around us and establish the Kingdom of God. Yet, according to this experiment, we are not allowed to have confidence.

This exercise showed that confidence, although essential for victorious living, has become a word the enemy has turned into a negative connotation for Christians today.

God knows that confidence is not only important, but it is a game changer in your life. That is why He encourages us to be confident.

As a challenge, let's see how confident are you today... in your relationships... in your finances... in your business... in the pursuit of your dreams... How about in God? If you take each of these categories and score it on a scale of 1-10 (1 being the lowest and 10 being the highest), where would you score?

Remember, Jesus didn't just conquer sin and the grave to just give you eternal life later; He did it to give you abundant life **now**. He didn't give His life so that you could score only 5's on your scale. Jesus is a 10, Jesus lives in you, and Jesus longs for you to be a 10 in all areas of your life.

That said, let's look at this confidence issue. Confidence can take a lifetime to build and establish, but only a few seconds to destroy. Why? Because confidence has to do with your belief: about God, about yourself, and about what God believes about you.

You need to understand that people who are confident carry a strong sense of self-worth. That does not mean they are self-centered, but that they have an understanding of their value.

Do you understand your value, your worth? Here's a little reminder. God created you. He knows you, your value, and believes your value is so great that He gave His greatest treasure for you, so that He could be in relationship with you forever.

He has done everything He can to pursue you, encounter you, and demonstrate His goodness to you. He paid the price for anything that could ever slow you down or hinder your success because He sees great value in you. He longs for everyone around you to see the value, the worth, and the treasure that He sees in you.

The challenge is for you to see yourself the way God sees you. He doesn't see your flaws and your sins; He sees the treasure in you.

The problem is when we determine our value based on how others view us and not on how God views us. We tend to look for our value from those around us, those we interact with, and not from One who created us and knows us best.

Children who are extremely confident usually come from a home where parents tell them that they can achieve anything. If you say it often enough they start to believe it. If you reinforce it enough, they start to live it.

God has not only shown your value, but He reminds you that in Him nothing is impossible. Therefore you can boldly proclaim, "I can do all things through Christ who gives me strength." And, you can do ALL things. NOTHING is impossible. That sounds like a good father encouraging His child.

Some of us may have once had that confidence, but have since lost it because we have tried and failed. Thomas Edison said, "I didn't fail, I found 2,000 ways not to make a light bulb." But he only needed one to make it work.

A victorious life is about not focusing on how many times we fail, but seeing the victories that we have in Christ. If our confidence is in Christ Jesus, we cannot fail.

Paul, in Philippians 1:6 said to be confident. *Be confident of this, that He who has begun a good work in you will complete it.* Not only are we challenged to be confident, we are to live confidently.

Then Paul further challenges us by saying that the work that has begun in us is *good.* He wasn't encouraging them because everything was already going great. Paul was bringing this encouragement because they were struggling to know it was even good. When we struggle with what we have put our hand to and we lack the confidence, we begin to question not only the value of ourselves, but the value of what we are doing. Paul sets the record straight right here. Who you are is valuable and what you are doing is valuable. If you struggle with the understanding of who you are and your value, you will begin to question the value of those around you, your relationships, your marriage, your family, your job/workplace, not to mention the dreams and passions you are pursuing.

Today God wants to restore your confidence. He is actually challenging you to be confident. He wants to restore the value of what you are doing and pursuing and He is calling it *good*. Where have you had wrong beliefs that have lied to you, telling you that confidence is bad? Hand over those lies to God and ask Him replace them with truth of your value. Ask Him to show you where and in what ways you do not see the full value of you. Let Him open your eyes to the truth of your awesomeness.

Last, what areas do you want to begin to walk in greater confidence? What can you do today to begin to walk in that level of confidence in your relationships, in your work place, and in your community?

Remember, a victorious life is a confident life.

Challenge: Consider, then write down your responses:

1. Were you surprised by your scores regarding your confidence levels? Why or Why not?

2. Where have you believed lies, or has it been difficult to see the treasure God has placed in you?

3. Where has it been difficult to see the value of those around you?

Prayer: "God, I break off the lie that I am not of high worth, that I am not valuable. I pray today that You will begin to reveal to me an understanding of how You see me. Please open my eyes to my value to You and Your great love for me. Show me what You love about me, and what You value in me. I declare today that the works I have started are *good*. My relationships are *good*, my family is *good*, the dream for my life is *good*. I place my confidence in You, my trust in You, knowing that You are a good and loving God. Today I will not be discouraged and I will not be brought down. Thank you that today I will walk in the confidence of a great God, and today I will live victoriously. In Jesus' name, Amen."

CHALLENGE
— 12 —

IN THE MIDNIGHT HOUR

- ACTS 16:25-26 -

About midnight Paul and Silas were praying and singing hymns to God, and the other prisoners were listening to them. Suddenly there was such a violent earthquake that the foundations of the prison were shaken. At once all the prison doors flew open, and everyone's chains came loose.
Acts 16:25-26

I often hear, "You are the same when you are preaching on the stage as you are in the business you own, and as you are around the fire pit in your backyard." Good or bad, I hear it.

For some people, that is **not** what they are looking for. They want a Pastor who is different, who is pious and reserved and doesn't mingle with the local folk. For me, it is one of the greatest compliments! It is also a reminder to me that people are watching. I choose to live my life out in the open. My good days, bad days, triumphs and failures are all out there to be seen. I want those around me to see that the power of my God is not a concept, it is the real deal.

At the beginning of Acts 16, Paul and Silas are on their way to pray... on their way to church service. They had good intentions to do a good thing when their day gets hijacked. They help a poor demon possessed girl they meet along the way. Next thing you know, they are stripped, beaten, flogged and thrown into a prison cell. I have had days like that. Well, maybe not where I've been publicly stripped and beaten, but days where it sure has felt that bad.

Then Paul and Silas do something amazing. When it is darkest, when hope would be the most distant, at about the midnight hour, they begin to sing praises to God. When it seemed the most impossible they began to Praise God.

How you respond when it is darkest is the truest reveal of your relationship with God. How you respond in your midnight hour is key to living a life of victory.

Paul and Silas began to praise. Let me tell you what praise does. It shifts the focus from your problem to your solution. Praise declares the power, goodness, and authority of your God to you, and to your problem. Praise isn't a reminder to God of how great He is. Praise is a reminder to you. When you begin to praise, you start elevating your faith to supernatural levels.

Psalms 23 says that God is inhabited in the praises of His people. Praise is an invitation to the almighty God to come and be a part of your solution. It creates an atmosphere of Heaven where the presence of God resides. Where the presence of God is, there is power. Where the power of God is, nothing can stay the same.

If you want to see true transformation in some of the darkest times of your life, begin to praise. It transforms your outlook, and invites God to partner with you for supernatural change in what you are facing.

Instead of focusing on your lack, begin to praise God for being a God of abundance. Instead of focusing on your infirmity, begin to praise God that by Christ's stripes you are healed. Instead of focusing on the impossibilities of your situation, begin to praise God that in Him nothing is impossible. Begin to remind yourself of what He has done and who He says that He is. It is hard to stay in a place of doubt when you are speaking and singing the praises of a faithful God.

That being said, the miraculous does not stop there. The other prisoners were listening.

The world does not care how you respond when everything is going right. They want to know how you are going to respond when it is darkest, when you are facing the same things they are facing. The friends who are closest to me do not want to know what my sermon was about on Sunday. They want to know how I am going to deal with Monday... just like them.

Paul and Silas found themselves in the same situation as the other prisoners, beaten and shackled.

Yet they found a hope and began to praise. To the astonishment of everyone around them, they began to glorify God.

The world is watching you. They are not as interested in you having millions of dollars as they are curious about how you will deal with lack. They are not concerned if you have a perfect marriage; they are watching to see how you handle your arguments. Your neighbors, those you witness to, those you are in relationship with, are watching to see how you handle disappointment, discouragement, failure, bad news, and bad days.

When Paul and Silas praised God it brought supernatural power into their situation. As they praised, a violent earthquake shook the prison cell, the doors flew open and everyone's chains came off.

Two amazing things happen here. **The doors flew open.** In your life if you are facing some closed doors: in business, in finance, or in relationships, start praising God. Remember, *as* they praised God, closed doors opened.

Then it says that everyone's chains came off. Not just Paul and Silas, **everyone**! Their freedom was everyone's freedom. Their breakthrough was everyone's breakthrough. Their victory was everyone's victory.

What God is doing (and wanting to do) in and through you is not just for you, but for those around you. You might not even realize it, but your freedom could bring freedom for your family, or for your kids. Your victory could be a victory for your spouse, friends, or workplace. Yes, God wants to give you victory for you, but He also wants that victory for everyone around you.

Talk about a powerful testimony.

Talk about the power of Praise.

In the midst of whatever you are facing today, choose to begin praising God and see doors open in your life.

What does that look like? It looks like glorifying Him, no matter what. In the face of those things you struggle and battle with most, give God praise. Invite God to partner with you in victory.

Remember... Praise is a key part of a victorious life.

Challenge: Consider, then write down your responses:

1. Where have you been focused on the problem, instead of the solution?
2. Where have others been watching to see how you handle your midnight times?
3. Is there any area where you feel chained, or cannot find a hope? Ask God to show you how to praise Him in the face of the struggle.

Prayer: "Today God, I choose to give You praise. I glorify You and all that You have done in my life. Thank You for redeeming me and restoring me. There is no one like You, God, in all of the heavens and the earth. I magnify Your Name. I invite You into my struggles and my battles. I declare that You are my victory and that You are my hope. I release your supernatural power into every area of my life: my finances, my relationships, my workplace, my dreams and my destiny. Today, I declare freedom not only for myself, but for those around me, and anyone I come into contact with. Today, I choose to walk in victory with You. In Jesus' name, Amen."

CHALLENGE
— 13 —

THE POWER OF PRESENCE

- EXODUS 33:15-16 -

*Then Moses said to him, "If your Presence does not
go with us, do not send us up from here. How will
anyone know that you are pleased with me and with
your people unless you go with us? What else will
distinguish me and your people from all the other
people on the face of the earth?"*
Exodus 33:15-16

I had a professor in Bible school who always said
"Presence = Power." He explained that in the Bible,
anywhere you saw the presence of God it equated to
the power of God.

I have had times in my life where I would have
preferred to separate the two. There have been
moments when I would like the power of God in my
life, but wasn't sure I wanted His presence to be

active right then. I wanted God to move in power and shift a situation or bring resources where there was lack; I just didn't want to take the time to nurture my relationship with Him. The presence of God can be inconvenient when our agenda is different than His.

Power is the expression of God while presence is the nature of God. One is the *result of* who He is; the other is *intimacy with* who He is.

I have attended many Charismatic Christian conferences where they trained people in the spiritual gifts. Typically, instruction focused heavily on the power of God, the expression of who He is, with little focus on nurturing the presence of God.

The level of our desire (pursuit) for God's presence or for His power when life situations happen, reveals the state of our heart.

In Exodus 33, Moses is given the opportunity to have the power without the presence. God actually tells Moses that He will send an angel with Moses and God will drive out the enemy before him. That sounds like a pretty awesome offer. Yet Moses contends with God for more.

First, Moses seems to have a solid revelation of *Presence = Power*. He tells God, *"If your Presence does not go with us, do not send us up from here.* He is not willing to settle for an angel. Moses does not simply want the result; He wants the presence of God.

Second, Moses knows that the presence of God is the distinguishing mark on the people of God. He asks, *What else will distinguish me and your people from all the other people on the face of the earth?*

It is important to note that the people of God should always be marked by the power of God. His power should be a distinguishing mark on our daily lives.

How does the power of God look in your life? What does it look like in your relationships?

For the Israelites, they could be identified by the cloud that went before them by day and the fire God provided by night. People probably never questioned their power because they could actually see it.

How is the real, tangible power of God revealed in your life? It could be you loving the unlovable, or forgiving the unforgivable. It could be seeing healings, miracles, or outrageous faith.

Think of the ways people around you can see God's presence in and through you. Do you want more? Ask God to show you how to cultivate a deeper relationship with Him so that there would be distinguishing marks on your daily life.

What would a deeper relationship look like with God? Have there been areas of your life where you know God has been pursuing a deeper relationship with you, but you have not said, "Yes" to Him?

Let God know now that you want His presence. You want to know it is real, tangible, and visible-to-those-around-you. Tell Him you want His presence AND His power.

My favorite part of Exodus 33 is Moses' final request. It is the request the reveals his nature, his true heart for God. In Verse 18 Moses asks God to, *Show me Your face, show me Your glory.*

It is as if Moses is saying, "As much as I love seeing Your power in my life, I want Your presence. I want to know You more."

Moses' true heartbeat, His deep heart's desire was for the presence of God, the nature of God in his life.

You may need to see the power of God in your life or your situations today. And you can. But His presence is so much sweeter.

Challenge: Consider, then write down your responses:

1. Have their been times when you would have rather had God's power than His presence?
2. How would others say you are marked by God?

3. What has held you back from pursuing a deeper relationship with God?

Prayer: "Today, God, I cry out to You: do not take me from this place unless Your presence goes with me. I want Your presence in my home, my workplace, my school, my city and my region. Allow Your presence to be a defining mark on my life, my family, and my dreams. Allow my life to showcase the power of a good God. Give me opportunities today to display Your power, to reveal Your healing, to share Your love. Today, God, I long for more. I long to see Your face, to see Your glory, and to encounter You. Take me deeper in You, Lord. Be revealed to me and in me. Today, Lord, I celebrate that in Your presence is the power that makes me victorious. In Jesus' name, Amen."

CHALLENGE
— 14 —
FULLY RESTORED
- JOEL 2:25-26 -

So I will restore to you the years that the swarming locust has eaten, the crawling locust, the consuming locust, and the chewing locus. My great army which I sent among you, you shall eat in plenty and be satisfied, and praise the name of the LORD your God, who has dealt wondrously with you; and My people shall never be put to shame.
Joel 2:25-26

The promise in Joel 2 is exciting! What a great and powerful promise we have from God. Not only does God say that He is going to restore the years that have been taken from us, this also includes the years that were taken because of our own disobedience. (Ouch!) Then He says that we shall eat in plenty and be satisfied. He promises that we shall be full, no longer in want, and that we shall not be put to shame. That means we will be restored, better than before, fully satisfied with no shame. Talk about a good day!

We have all experienced loss in some way or another: in relationships, finances, loss in careers. In Joel 2:25, God is specifically talking about the loss of years. We can believe for the above-mentioned things being restored. The idea of finances or relationships being restored can seem easier for us to wrap our head around than the idea of years being restored. We can believe in the restoration of items much easier than we can believe in the restoration of time.

Joel starts by writing about a great loss more devastating than the people had ever been through before. In Joel 1:4, he writes about the chewing locust, the swarming locust, the crawling locust, the consuming locust. That is a lot of locust; as in locust on top of locust, on top of locust. He even asks them, have you ever been through anything like this before? Have you ever heard of anything like this before in your life?

This makes what happened with Moses and the plagues feel like amateur hour. He was not writing about just a one-time, one-day experience. It was year after year after year. The locust where so numerous, so thick, they would literally blot out the sun and darkness would completely engulf the land. Some of us know what that feels like. These locusts would consume every bit of grain in the field leaving nothing behind but what appeared to be desolate, scorched earth... it looked like a complete loss.

I have people tell me all the time, "You have no idea what I am going through." Or, "No one has ever had it as bad as me." You are probably right and I don't even have to argue with you to tell you that God's promise applies to you. It doesn't matter how bad it is or if it is the worst that has ever been, God still has a promise for you. I also have people tell me that it is their own fault when bad things happen. That could be true, but God still promises to restore.

For the Israelites, this loss of the crops wasn't just allocated to food. This affected every aspect of their lives, including their finances and their economy. They were not able to feed their families, let alone livestock. It affected their ability to bring grain sacrifices to the Lord, which affected their relationship with God. Once crops were destroyed and food became scarce, it likely lowered immune systems and affected health. This destruction, the loss of years, affected every aspect of their lives. Then God gave a promise. He said, *I will restore. I will fill your threshing floors with new crops and your vats shall overflow with new wine.*

Many have experienced such a deep, personal, life-shaking loss that life feels hopeless. Some have lost relationships, where it has affected every part of their lives, year after year. Others have experienced loss in business where it affects their resolve or confidence to risk again. Loss can affect our personal finances and leave us feeling broken and in despair. Loss due to sickness may erode strength, sap finances and leave us feeling hollow and depressed. Maybe you have had loss that has affected your family, your loved ones, or available time with friends.

Despite how painful that loss is, or the fact that no one may have ever experienced what you have gone (or are currently going) through, God still gives you a promise, *I will restore*.

What a great and powerful promise. God does not say there is a *chance* He will restore, He says that He **will** restore. You will not have to fight for it, contend for it, beg for it, or struggle to obtain it. He will do it. He is the one who restores.

God longs to generously pour out so many blessings upon you and your life that you will eat until you can no longer eat another bite. He longs for you to be satisfied and full in Him. He doesn't want you to just have relationships, He wants those relationships to be on such a satisfying, intimate level that they restore you and fill you up. He wants you to have more than a job. He wants your job to be an opportunity for Him to express His fullness in your life in a way that gives you so much joy and peace that it blesses others around you. He doesn't just want to heal your loneliness or depression, He wants to break off any and all shame in your life altogether.

God gives us this great promise of restoration to give us hope and to lift us up. But like most promises there is a challenge and a responsibility on our part. The love of God is unconditional, but His promises are conditional.

In Joel 2:12, He lays out the challenge. Remember, God says He will restore. Since He is the One who will be doing the restoring, our part is to partner with Him. *Now, therefore, says the Lord, turn to me with all your heart...* God longs to restore everything that has been lost or destroyed in our lives, but He is asking us to partner with Him wholly. He says *turn to Me* with all of you. This includes your focus, attention, affection, and your whole heart. So often, after experiencing heartbreaking loss, we stay focused on the loss, instead of the restorer. Or we stay focused on our pain instead of the healer. How often do we focus on our lack instead of our source?

What losses have you experienced? Have you lost finances, relationships, a job, a dream, or maybe years? Ask God to reveal to you how and where He has been helping, healing, supporting, or providing for you during this time. How has He revealed His love for you in this season? Who has He placed in your life to help you journey the process of grief? Then, ask Him to fill your threshing floors with new crops and your vats to overflowing. He may have to first heal your heart. If that is the case, invite Him to heal you in the broken places. He will!

The heart is the core of our whole being: spirit, soul and body. It is the life source for our relationships, dreams, and passions. It leads us and directs us. God is reminding us to turn our full attention and focus onto Him. That is where we will find the power, restoration and transformation we seek. The heart is where God begins to restore the years… in us… to us… and through us.

Our victory in Him is not in our ability to get it all right all of the time. God knows and understands when our hearts go astray. Our victory comes from knowing where to turn our heart when we get it wrong, and how to partner with God daily in our lives so that we can live victoriously!

Challenge: Consider, then write down your responses:

1. What are you still waiting for God to restore, that was taken or destroyed in your life?
2. What would the restoration of years look like in your life?
3. In your loss, how has it been difficult to turn your whole heart to God?

Prayer: "Today God, I turn my whole heart, my whole attention, my full focus onto You. Be my restorer and my all-in-all. I ask for forgiveness for those times and places when I have tried to do it on my own. I need You in my life - today and always. Today, God, I ask You to restore the years that have been lost, the joy that has been eroded, the peace that has been taken, and the love that has been tarnished. Fill me up, Lord, today. I long to be live fully satisfied in my life and in my walk with You. I break off any remnant of shame and any lie of the enemy. I release the fullness of Your goodness in my life. I partner with You, God, as you fully restore me and my life in every way. I choose today to be victorious in You. In Jesus' name, Amen."

CHALLENGE
— 15 —

GET YOUR HOPES UP

- ROMANS 15:13 -

*May the God of hope fill you with all joy and
peace as you trust in Him, so that you may overflow
with hope by the power of the Holy Spirit.*
Romans 15:13

"I hope that one day I can ride a bike like the big
kids," my son, Evan, said as he saw his two older
sisters riding bikes around our neighborhood. He
was much younger, and though he had a bike, he
didn't want a bike with training wheels. He hoped
to ride a bike free and unencumbered like his sisters,
like the big kids.

That hope was a driving force. Here was this little
guy watching his sisters go round and round. The
more he watched, the more he wanted it, and the
more he would say, "I hope, one day…"

When I checked on the kids again, I found that Evan had taken the training wheels off his bike and was dragging it towards the street. That *one day* was going to be *today*, in his mind.

"What are you doing?" I asked. He looked at me with eyes that said, "Who, me?" He was determined to ride like the big kids. Not too much later that same day, he figured out how to ride that bike. There were a few crashes, scrapes and bruises, but none of that deterred him. He was determined to be victorious and it all started with HOPE.

I heard that same hope talked about in a church some time back. Not as a sermon, a message, or even from the pulpit, but from a little girl. She came forward for prayer for healing saying, "I hope that God heals me today." She had seen others get healed in that very service. She wanted to get healed *like the big kids*. It was from that altar, from that young girl that I heard hope talked about, then crushed. "You don't have to hope, we know that God heals." The altar worker thought they were being an encourager, but instead deflated the tender hope of this young girl. I wanted to yell, "No! Get your hopes up!"

How has hope become such a bad word and mindset in the church? We stir up faith, we nurture love, we encourage strong belief, but we seldom even talk about hope.

Paul tells us in 1st Corinthians that these three remain: faith, hope and love. Hope is one of the three key things that remain. It is pretty important. If the devil can kill hope, then we will seldom get to faith. Hope is a faith igniter.

The definition of hope is, "a feeling of expectation." I have heard it said so many times, "Don't get your hopes up." But Christ wants you to, "Get your HOPES up!" "Raise your expectations!"

Romans 15:13 says that the God of hope wants you to overflow with hope. He doesn't just want you to have it, He wants you to have it in such abundance that it overflows in your life. Then everyone around you gets a taste of hope.

Romans 8:25 says, *But if we hope for what we do not see, we eagerly wait for it with perseverance.* This scripture tells us that if we raise our expectations and do not see the answer yet, we should pursue it without letting go. This passage challenges us to passionately pursue hope with vigilance. That is the power of hope in our life.

Proverbs 13:12 says, *Hope deferred makes the heart sick, but a longing fulfilled is a tree of life.* We all have experienced the heartbreak of hope deferred, or failed expectations. The first half of this scripture may be familiar, but the second half is where the power lies. Longing fulfilled is a tree of life. As Christians, we get to raise our expectations to supernatural levels. Then, as we get our hopes up, God meets us there and we become a source of life to all those around us. The encouragement here is not just to hope. It is to remind us that because our hope is in God, we hope differently. Our great expectation that God will meets us in the midst of our circumstances becomes life for others. The power of our testimony then spurs others to get their hopes up, too.

How does hope happen? Well, Romans tells us that *the God of hope will fill you with joy and peace as you trust in Him so that you may overflow with hope.*

It starts with trusting in Him. As you trust in God, He fills you with a peace that surpasses understanding. That peace gives you joy in any situation you are facing. It allows and frees you to get your hopes up, so that you may overflow with hope. Hope has to start with trusting... in Him. As your trust grows, your hope grows.

It may be that you have fallen down, been bruised or scraped by life's circumstances, or by the unsuccessful pursuit of your dreams and desires. Maybe you have been hurt in relationships, by family, by those you care about most. Perhaps that hurt has affected your ability to trust or killed your hope. God wants to restore you today. He longs for you to draw near to Him, so He can restore right understanding of your value, of your view of Him as a loving Father, and your view of you as a child of the King. He is restoring your desire to seek Him, pursue Him, and your rights as a son or daughter of the King. He doesn't just want you to draw near just so you are nearer, He wants to restore your trust in Him. When you fall down, and you will, He wants to pick you up and say, "Try again."

Are there areas where you have fallen down or have no hope (or little hope)? Are there areas where you struggle with peace, with joy, or with your ability to trust God? Remember, God—the God of hope—wants to fill you so full of joy and peace that you will overflow with hope. If that sounds like a good deal, just tell Him, "Yes!"

Victorious living is not just about having the huge one-day victory, but about not giving up. Sometimes your victory comes from just getting back up, or from getting your hopes up.

Challenge: Consider, then write down your responses:

1. Where is God wanting you to get your hopes up?

2. In what areas has it been difficult to receive peace?

3. Where is God wanting you to "try again?"

Prayer: "Heavenly Father, today I draw near to You, close to You, and I seek Your face. Restore in me a greater level of trust: in You, in Your plan and Your will for my life. I want to trust that You love me unconditionally and that You will never leave me. Pour out in me a supernatural level of peace that surpasses what I am facing today. Let that peace surpass my worry, doubt or fear today. Give me new levels of joy to celebrate what You are doing in my life, my family, and my dreams today. Today, God, I get my hopes up in You! I raise my expectations to supernatural levels and expect today is going to be a great day of victory as I live victoriously in You, the God of hope. In Jesus' name, Amen."

VICTORIOUS

CHALLENGE
— 18 —

YOU'VE GOT WHAT YOU NEED

- EPHESIANS 1:3 -

Praise be to the God and Father of our Lord Jesus Christ, who has blessed us in the heavenly realms with every spiritual blessing in Christ.
Ephesians 1:3

Hardware stores are profitable because they know you do not have what you need, and their store does. And, they know a secret: you will never get everything you need for your project the first time you visit the store. How do I know? All I wanted to do was paint one wall in one room.

First step, go to the hardware store. If you are like me, you don't even bother with a list. It was a simple job... I needed paint, brushes, rollers and I should be good to go.

While at the hardware store, I decided to also pick up light bulbs, a new screw driver, and a plant for my wife. What should have cost $40, now cost $100. No problem.

When I get home, I realize I am missing a tarp for the paint and primer. So I head back to the hardware store. I figured I might as well pick up that new drill while I'm there. I get back home and I am ready; I have everything. Wait, there are cracks in the wall, and holes from pictures previously hung. I make a quick run back out, I just need plaster and putty. But I might as well pick up a few boards just in case I am going to build something sometime. It's the hardware store trap. Five visits to the hardware store, hundreds of dollars later, I now have things I don't really need. I am now too tired to paint a wall, so I decide to leave it the color that it was.

How often do we do we approach other areas of our life with "I just need..."? In business, we need just one more client or one more sale. In finances, just one more deposit or one more month. In relationships, we just need one more chance.

"I just need more..." implies you don't have what you need. In our spiritual life it can sound like, "God, I just need a little more grace." "God, I just needed a little more patience, for my kids, for my work, or for my spouse." "God I just needed a little more love, then I would have forgiven them, treated them nicer, turned the other cheek." You can feel like you just don't have everything you need to make today a victorious day.

When those *not enough* days happen, we usually point a finger, but not at our self. That can make it our spouse's fault, our boss's fault, the bookkeeper's fault, or the economy's fault. In church it can be the pastor's fault for not preaching the message you wanted or needed. Or it can be the worship team's fault for not singing your favorite song. It certainly seems easier to blame the *not enough* in your life on someone else.

Here is where I have some good news and some tough news for you.

The good news is that God has given you everything you need to be victorious today. Notice that I **didn't** say successful. Your success and your victory may look like very different things.

While I am a multi-trip-to-the-hardware-store kind of guy, my father in-law is a different story. When I visit his home to help him with different projects, we never leave the house. In his garage he has every tool, every item, and numerous contraptions I didn't even know existed. We could be painting a wall when a water pipe bursts. He would say, "Matthew, just go into the garage, I've got something for that." We could be planting some plants when the gas main goes. "Matthew, just check the garage, I have a thing for that." We could be fixing a fence and the roof cave in. "Matthew, no worries, I have just what we need."

No matter how random or crazy the crisis, his blood pressure never rises, his voice never wavers, he has full confidence. Why? He is equipped and he knows it. Imagine living life that way, with that kind of assurance.

Paul tells us in Ephesians that we get to praise God because He has blessed us with every spiritual blessing. How many blessings did He bless us with? Every one! That is a lot of spiritual blessings.

God has equipped you today with everything you need to be victorious. Where has He blessed you? In heavenly places. Why is this important? It is common to feel that if our resource is in heavenly places then it is just out of reach for us.

You may feel like, "Sorry God, You should have put those resources in earthly places and then I would have had access to them." Nope. He places them in heavenly places.

Remember that prayer that Jesus taught His disciples to pray: *Our Father, who art in Heaven hollowed be Thy name. Thy Kingdom come Thy will be done on Earth as it is in Heaven...* On Earth as it is in Heaven. This prayer is challenging... Heaven on Earth?

The first part of the challenge is to believe that it is possible and that God wants to. If Heaven on Earth is possible, that means no more excuses. That is the tough news. No more trips to the spiritual hardware store.   Instead, we are challenged to have full confidence that what we need is there when we need it.

What does Heaven on Earth look like? It happens when we push through *I need more* to ***I've got what I need***.

"God, I just need a little more grace." God says, "In Me you have limitless grace and My grace is sufficient."

"God, I just need a little more peace to make it through the day. You don't know what was just thrown at me, or what I am facing right now." God responds with, "My peace surpasses your understanding of what you are facing today."

"God, I just need more love today. My love tank is empty." God reminds us that nothing separates us from His love and that His love is never ending.

"God, my roof just caved in, the water main just blew, and my internal gasket is going." God says, "Don't worry, don't raise your voice, and don't lose your peace, your patience, or your grace. I have just what you need when you need it."

We may be looking for God to fill our tank with just enough of what we need for the week. At the same time, we fear we may run out depending on what we face.

God is a limitless source that we get to plug into, connect with every day, every moment, and every breath of our life.

He is our endless supply, and a constant source of power that never runs out or runs dry.

The Bible is full of promises of His love and abundant provision for us. Once we stop making excuses, then we start making room... for Heaven on Earth. Then we can say, "God, I invite You into every area and aspect of my life." That is when we start establishing Heaven on Earth, seeing His Kingdom come, and always walking in a new level of being equipped with everything we need, when we need it.

Consider areas of your life (spiritual, emotional, relational, financial, and physical) where you believe that you lack or *don't have enough.* Now, ask God to show you what, how and where He has provided or given you what you need in the moment of need. Ask Him where His grace has been sufficient for what you have been going through.

The victory in Christ comes from knowing that God has equipped you with everything you need today for what you will face. You will be able to say with confidence, **"I've got what I need**." That is victorious living.

Challenge: Consider, then write down your responses:

1. Is there any area where you have blamed "not enough" on someone else?
2. Is there any place your love tank feels empty? Ask God to fill it up.
3. Do you have full confidence that what you need will be there when you need it?

Prayer: "Today, Lord, I thank You and give You praise that You have equipped me with everything I need to walk in victory. I do not live in lack or less. Help me to see that I have all I need and I can live in abundance in You. I pray Heaven on Earth in my life. I choose to partner with a good God in all of my passions and pursuits. Today, God, I press into You as my resource for my relationships, family, ideas and strategies. Thank You that in and through You, God, I have an endless supply of Your goodness manifested in my life. I break off any lies or doubts from the enemy that say I will not have enough or that I will be left in want. I press fully into the truth of my loving God. Today, I choose to walk in victory no matter what comes my way! In Jesus' name, Amen."

VICTORIOUS

CHALLENGE
— 17 —

MORE

- EPHESIANS 3:20 -

*Now to Him who is able to do immeasurably
more than all we ask or imagine, according
to His power that is at work within us.*
Ephesians 3:20

"Please sir, I want some more." This famous line is from a young orphan boy named Oliver in Charles Dickens' tale, Oliver Twist. Oliver brings his worn wooden bowl up to the Head Master and asks for a refill of his gruel. The Head Master, standing proud in his chef apron, is shocked and outraged. As Oliver says again, "I want some more," the Head Master beats him down with his ladle for perceived insolence.

Have you ever felt like the young orphan bringing your wooden bowl up to a church altar in asking for just one more touch, or one more healing prayer before being brought down with, "You should be happy with what you have?" I have heard that line shared so many times that it has become, sadly, more famous to me than the words young Oliver uttered to his Head Master.

Longing, wanting, or believing for more, has become something of a negative or offensive ideology. That is why we have conditioned ourselves to be okay with what we have, and learned to settle with what has been given us. But that leaves us living with less than the fullness of what God wants to do in our life. We have believed a lie that tells us to *make do* with what we have.

We have a God of ***more***! God longs to do *more*—immeasurably more—in our life, finances, relationships, business, and in our region. Our God of endless resources longs for us to want more, and then ask for more, so He can pour it out. Sounds easy, right?

On the surface, most of us would be in agreement and nod our head that, "Okay, God longs to give us more." Many may believe that the idea of *more* is okay. But to truly walk in the victory of **more**, we might have to change years of preconditioned thinking.

For many years, I lived discouraged even though I believed I had a God who would meet my needs. Seldom did God move when I wanted Him to, almost never did He work within my time table, but He did always met my needs.

I was encouraged by a pastor friend to be happy that at least God was meeting my needs. Hmmmm. Something wasn't lining up. I didn't want to just barely eke by in life. My life was supposed to be a testimony to the greatness of a great God. The more I have understood who God is, the more I have realized I was settling for a version of God that wasn't the God He wanted to be in my life. I don't serve a God of just enough, I serve a God of **more** than enough.

That is when God gave me a revelation, "I meet needs, but I surpass expectations." Then He challenged me, "Which are you bringing to Me?"

Was I bringing God my needs or was I bringing God my expectations? Was I bringing Him my list of my essentials to just barely get by today, or was I partnering with God in my dreams, ideas, passions for the above and beyond?

God doesn't just want to be our needs supplier; He wants to partner with us for **more**! The powerful word there is *more*! He wants to see us come alive with big, loud, colorful, powerful living, not just getting by. He is the God of *more*. Not just a plain old simple *more*, but of **immeasurably** *more*. That means that the *more* that He wants to do is so massive and amazing that it cannot be measured.

What would that kind of *more* look like in your life, your family, your dreams or pursuits? What would *more* look like in your finances or your health? God wants to do what He can imagine, it is *immeasurably more than you can imagine*.

How do you walk in the *more*? First, you have to be able to believe that He longs to do more in your life. Imagine it. Next you get to ask for it.

There has been an all-out assault on imagination. In the church, not only has the idea of *more* and longing for more been treated as bad, but the imagination has been all but outlawed. Imagination has been branded worldly and sinful by many for a long time. When you finally do get the understanding that God does want to do more in your life, without imagination it can be limited to what you can see. That does not factor in that God moves in the unseen, or that faith is the product of what you don't see.

You were made in God's image. He created you. He has made you with a mind has the amazing ability to create thoughts... imaginative thoughts. He didn't give you an imagination so that you would never use it. In fact, all technological and scientific advances have come from those who first conceived (imagined) the idea. You get to imagine supernatural possibilities with God; the same God who created Heaven and the Earth.

God wants to surpass your expectations and partner with you to create opportunity for your *more* to become a reality.

Ephesians 3:20 reminds us that *more* happens through the power already at work within us.

Allow God's power to work *more* within you. It is then that you'll move from the *idea* of victory to victoriously living.

A victorious life is one that can partner with God's power and **His** idea of what victory can look like in your life.

Challenge: Consider, then write down your responses:

1. Where have you learned to make do with what you have?
2. What is the most outrageously large *more* you can imagine for your life?
3. What areas of your life has it been difficult to really believe God wants you to live in the abundant *more*?

Prayer: "God, I thank You that You are holy, powerful, mighty and that there is no one else like You. Thank You that I get to partner with Your power in my life. Today, God, I raise my expectations and stir my imagination to supernatural levels. I release the *more* of Heaven into my life. I break off any limits I have believed about the immeasurable *more* You have for me in my relationships, my finances, my work place, my dreams and my pursuits. I will not come into agreement with doubt, lack, fear or worry. I know that You, God, have *more* for me today. I choose today to live in victory and allow the *more* of my life to testify to a victorious God. In Jesus' name, Amen."

VICTORIOUS

- NEHEMIAH 1:11 -

*Lord, let Your ear be attentive to the prayer
of this Your servant and to the prayer of Your
servants who delight in revering Your name.
Give Your servant success today by granting
him favor in the presence of this man.*
Nehemiah 1:11

I was driving with my children one day in a mad
dash to get to a store before it closed. I have always
believed that traffic lights know when you are in a
hurry because the more you need a light to turn or
stay green, the more likely it will be red.

On this particular day, in my hurry to get to this
store, every light turned green. It felt amazing, like
the waters parting for Moses. It was supernatural!
It was a miracle! It was the favor of God. I even

said it out loud, "The favor of God is on me!" It only took my daughter a second to say, "Dad. That is not how favor works." Really? That is not how favor works? Then how does it work? What does God's favor in our life look like?

I absolutely believe that the people of God are supposed to be a people marked by favor. Most would probably agree. However, if we don't know what favor looks like, we won't know what we are praying or contending for.

Nehemiah personally contended for his victory. Before he had a meeting with the king, he prayed God would grant him favor. He knew that favor was important and he also knew that God could give it to him.

The favor of God on Nehemiah's life opened a door for him to meet with the King, who had an attentive ear, a receptive heart and a willingness to partner with Nehemiah's passion. He didn't just get to meet with the King, but the King was willing to listen, was understanding and agreed to the request Nehemiah made.

That is pretty amazing when you consider that Nehemiah was just a servant, a cup bearer. That is some powerful favor.

The favor of God on your life opens doors that appear impossible. It can transform your status, increase your influence, and release supernatural resources.

David declared the favor of God in Psalms 90:17, *Let the favor of the Lord our God be upon us, and establish the work of our hands upon us; yes, establish the work of our hands!* Let the favor of God be upon us? When is the last time you prayed for the favor of God to be demonstrated in your life? What would His favor look like manifested in everything you do?

I love this definition of favor: demonstrated delight. Favor is God's demonstrated delight... it can look like green traffic lights, or an open door to meet with the King.

When I first saw Siobhan, my wife, she captured my heart, my attention, and my love. It wasn't enough that I knew it internally, I wanted her to know it. I wanted everyone to know it. She was my everything. So I favored her, in every way that I could. I gave her more attention than anyone else, bought her gifts, and paid for her meals. My focus was on her, so I demonstrated delight in her every opportunity that I had.

As much as my love for my wife is great, God's love for us is even greater. How much more does He favor us? How much more does He long to demonstrate His delight over us?

The Bible says that Jesus not only had favor, but He increased in favor, with both God and man. Luke 2:52, *And Jesus increased in wisdom and in stature and in favor with God and man.* Luke says that Jesus increased in favor with God and with man. That means the delight of God was on Him.

It is not hard for us to imagine the delight of God on His Son, but can you imagine the delight of the Lord on you? Did you know that He delights in all that you do, in all that you put your hand to?

Today, what would change if the delight of the Lord, the favor of God, was on your relationships? How would your work place, job, and passions be if His delight was on them? How would you live if you walked in the true understanding that God's delight IS upon everything you place your hand to? If Jesus (God's Son) was able to increase in favor, then as God's sons and daughters, we can too.

Consider what the favor of God looks like in your life. What would the favor of man look like in your life? What can you do to grow in favor with those around you? Thank God for the favor He has granted you, then ask Him to pour out and saturate every area of your life with even more favor.

Your victory is not found in your ability, but in the Lord's delighting, in His favor upon you.

Challenge: Consider, then write down your responses:

1. What relationship are you most contenting for favor?

2. What would that favor look like?
3. In what way has this challenge taught you or encouraged you regarding God's favor?

Prayer: "In my life today, Lord I pray that You will give me success and grant me victory by giving me favor. May Your delight be upon me and all that I put my hand to. Bless me outrageously with favor in my relationships, finances, home, work and pursuits. Help me to grow today in favor and wisdom with You, God. I long to fall more in love with You. Like Nehemiah, I pray that You would open the right doors for me and increase my influence in Your Kingdom wherever I go. May I grow in favor in my region so that I can see Your Kingdom come and Your will be done, today, on Earth as it is in Heaven. Teach me how to give favor to those around me in a way that reflects You well, Lord. Father, grant me victories today so that my life can be a declaration of a victorious life. In Jesus' name, Amen."

*See, I am doing a new thing! Now it springs up; do
you not perceive it? I am making a way in the
wilderness and streams in the wasteland.*
Isaiah 43:19

"For such a time as this..." Mordecai uttered these
powerful words to Esther, his cousin, the young girl
who he had brought in, cared for, and who had now
risen to be the Queen of the Persian Empire.
Mordecai challenged her to risk her life for the
Jewish people, her people.

Why was this such a risk? Esther was married to
the most ruthless king of the Persian nation, King
Xerxes. By a plot from the King's personal aid, a
decree had been sent out to kill all the Jews.
Though Esther wanted to help, she knew that

approaching the King without being summoned meant the risk of death. Not only were the lives of all the Jewish people on the line, Esther's own life was at stake.

Given the odds, crying out to God to remove her from the situation does not sound like a bad idea. Praying that God would give her a way out seems reasonable. Yet, Mordecai didn't pray a prayer for escape. Instead, he charged her with, *And who knows that you have come to your royal position for such a time as this.* His advice was framed upon, "Maybe God has placed you here for this moment. Maybe He doesn't want to give a way out as much as He wants to give a way through."

We love Esther's bravery as she risked it all to save her people. Not only did Esther not cry out to God for escape, she made a plan to fast, pray and risk. Her response? *If I die, I die...*

Have you ever been in an impossible, uncomfortable situation where you have prayed for God to take you out? What if that very circumstance is what God had called you to? Isaiah

142

43:19 promises that God is making a way in the wilderness, and streams in the wasteland (desert). But it doesn't promise God will take you from the wilderness, or remove you from the wasteland. Instead, God says He is going to transform it. That means your wilderness is no longer going to be a wilderness because He is making a way. Your desert place will no longer be a wasteland once it is flowing with fresh streams.

Sometimes we ask God to remove us from a place that He has called us to transform: a relationship, job, church or community. Or, we take ourselves out of that tough situation instead of being the answer to it. If Esther would have escaped in the midnight hour, people would have understood. But it would not have been the victory that God wanted for her and for His people.

I had an experience where my situation was so impossible I felt like I was sacrificing my life. My first prayer was, "God save me from this and get me out of here." Then God spoke to me, "If you go, who will pray in the new life? If you leave, who will establish my transforming power?"

What are you facing right now that you know God has been saying, "Let me make a way in this wilderness, let me bring new life to this dessert place."

Some relationships can feel like desert places, devoid of life. It can seem easier to begin to look for new relationships instead of declaring life in the relationships that we have. Many invest time, years, heart and soul into relationships only to give up on them when they feel dried up. God may be saying that you are there with purpose *for such a time as this* to declare and be a testimony of the transforming power of a good God.

Maybe your workplace, boss, or finances seem impossible. God is the God of the impossible. If you are praying for God to remove you and nothing has happened, maybe it is time start to pray that God moves **through** you. "God, allow me to be the new life that causes my workplace to come alive." "God, allow me to be the new life that causes my relationship/marriage/family to come alive." "God, today, let me be the change."

What areas in your life have you been crying out to God to remove you from? Maybe you just can't see a way through or how anything good can come from it. Invite God into these desert places, to make a way in the wilderness and create streams in the wasteland. Invite Him to do a new thing in and through you. Thank Him for the miracles that are on the way.

Note that this scripture in Isaiah begins with the declaration that God is doing a "new thing." It doesn't say, He is doing a "different thing." *Different* and *new* are not the same. Often what we really want God to do in our life is a *different* thing: a different job, different relationship, or a different church. Instead, what God is declaring is that He is doing something *new*. God is taking existing situations and doing new things with them. If you are only looking for something *different* you may just miss out on the *new* God is wanting to do in and through you.

Isaiah goes on to challenge, *do you not perceive it?* He encourages you to open your eyes and look because it is possible to miss what God is trying to do in your life. While you are looking for *different*, while you are looking elsewhere, while you are looking to move, change, shift, or give up, God says He is looking to do a miracle... right where you are.

Do you want to witness a miracle? Stay right in the midst of your impossible situation, Watch God make a way! The new life God is creating may happen suddenly... don't miss it! The way He is making is through **you**. The new life He is bringing is through **you**. The victory He is bringing is **your** victory, and it will bring victory to those around you.

When you partner with God to do a *new* thing, it leads to life and victorious living.

Challenge: Consider, then write down your responses:

1. Is there a particular wilderness or desert that God is challenging you to stay in and contend for a miracle in?

2. In what way can you see God's doing a *new* thing in you?

3. What in your life is God asking you to transform?

Prayer: "Today, God, I pray that You will open my eyes to see supernatural possibilities in my life. God, fill me with hope and strength to stand when I feel weak in the face of impossible odds. Let me be a way for those around me to experience Your victory. Let me be a source of new life in desert circumstances, to release new hope, joy and new levels of love. I declare over my relationships, my home, my workplace, and my job that they will be transformed into victorious environments that brings glory to You! Today, God, I lay ahold of the promise that I am here for such a time as this. I receive and release the new thing that You are doing and I partner with Your victory! In Jesus' name, Amen."

VICTORIOUS

CHALLENGE
— 20 —
PURSUIT

- 1 CORINTHIANS 14:1 -

Pursue love, and desire spiritual gifts,
1 Corinthians 14:1

Love is so powerful. Love relentlessly chased me down, pursued me, wooed me, and ultimately, won me. God's reckless, furious, sacrificial, scandalous love that can never be separated from me, is greater than anything I could imagine. It is a love that redeemed me, restored me, renewed me, set me up to succeed, and will never leave me.

God's love is so great that it believes all things - about my potential and every good possibility regarding who I am and my life. Love endures all things, including my failures, my faults, my missteps and misdeeds. This love hopes all things, which raises my expectations about me: who I am, and what I am capable of. It gives me room to be a better me, to grow, change, and develop without holding anything from the past against me. This great and powerful love that said no price was too great and no distance too far, sought me and won me.

God's great love is the doorway for eternal life. It is also the access point for life lived fully, abundantly, and victoriously.

As I read 1st Corinthians 14:1, God challenged me by asking, "Are you pursuing love? You know that you have received love, but are you pursuing love? In this scripture Paul tells us to *pursue* love, and *desire* spiritual gifts. God challenged me again, "How many times have you *pursued* spiritual gifts and only *desired* love.

Wow. Our entire social culture is built upon *desiring* love instead of *pursuing* it. And our whole Christian culture encourages *pursuing* spiritual gifts rather than *desiring* them. When was the last time you went to a Christian conference that just focused on the pursuit of love? Or a crusade just about pursuing love? If we were to stop and look at the top major conferences and retreats being promoted right now, they would likely be on evangelism, prophetic gifts, or healing ministries. None of those are bad, but are they cultivating a pursuit of love? In our life, are we fostering a pursuit of love?

Most of us would say we want to live a life that is victorious, powerful, transforming, and full of **all** the attributes and benefits of love. Yet, we spend our time pursuing anything but love. So do we actually desire love, or the product of love?

In relationships, true love will cultivate passionate romance. Yet, we often pursue the passionate romance and call it true love. Love creates an atmosphere of provision and protection, yet many pursue provision and protection then call it love.

Within love there is friendship and community, yet are we pursuing friendship and community, hoping it is love? Christ's love brings the promise of healing. Yet, we tend to pursue the gift of healing instead of His love.

Do you see what happens? Without realizing it, we can be running in the wrong direction, after the wrong thing. We are called to pursue the powerful love of God. As we abide in that place, healing, wholeness, power and victory are manifested in our lives. Do you want a fully victorious life? Ask God to help you pursue Him and His love.

Most days I am willing and open to love, but not necessarily pursuing it. After all, there are very real risks. In the Charismatic church we make room for the spiritual gifts. As we develop and grow in our Christianity, it is okay to risk big on the gifts, even if you fail. You are encouraged to pray for everyone who is sick. If only some get healed, that would be a wonderful victory. However, it seems that in love, in learning to love deeply, in putting your heart out there, you either have to win or you are out!

I am an avid comic book reader. In all the comic books I have ever read, usually the bad guy is pursuing powers and the good guy is giving it all for love. The bad guy is the one going after more abilities and special powers, while the good guy is struggling with the fact that he loves a world that will never love him back. They both receive their gifts, but whether and how they use them is an everyday choice.

We do the same. Paul tells us to *desire* gifts. After all, they are cool and God loves to give them out. But we are to *pursue* love: run after it, at all costs, with everything in us, chase love down. That is where our victory lies.

God's powerful love makes us victorious!

Challenge: Consider, then write down your responses:

1. What would an outrageous pursuit of God's love look like in your life today? What would change?
2. How would the fullness of revelation of His love shift your perspective today?
3. What is God calling you to do in the pursuit of love?

Prayer: "Thank You, God, for Your great love. Yours is a love that has surrounded me, redeemed me, restored me, healed me, made me whole, and never let me go. Today, God, I run after You and desire to pursue Your love in every area of my life. Let Your love that *believes* be manifested in me and my relationships. Let Your love that *hopes* be revealed through me and all that I put my hand to. Let Your love that *endures* be made powerful in me as I navigate the tough moments of my days. Let my life be a testimony to the greatness of Your love. Today, I choose to stand in the fullness of Your love. Thank You for the victory it gives me for abundant living now and for all eternity. Let Your love be showcased through me today as I live victoriously in You. In Jesus' name, Amen."

CHALLENGE
— 21 —

YOUR VICTORY

- ROMANS 8:37 -

Know in all these things we are more than
conquerors through Him who loved us.
Romans 8:37

They say that it takes a minimum of 21 days to make a habit, create a lifestyle, or to transform a pattern or way of thinking. Hopefully, by allowing yourself plenty of time to go through each of these Challenges, you have taken more than 21 days.

We hope this book has helped you begin to transform your mindsets, raised your expectations to supernatural levels of faith and belief, established a healthy expectation that God will move on your behalf today, and given you desire to partner with Him as He moves.

These 21 Challenges have been opportunities for you to raise your hopes, praise His name, pursue love, walk in His strength, and learn to live a victorious life.

We started these 21 Challenges in 1st Corinthians 15 declaring that we have the victory in Christ because He is our victor and through Him we get to partner with His victory.

Romans 8 tells us that in Him we are *more than* conquerors. A conqueror is someone who overcomes adversary. Paul was talking here to newly saved Roman citizens. The Romans had all seen someone overcome. They had seen someone be victorious. Paul takes it a step further and tells them that they are *more* than that. This applies to you, too. As a believer, you are not just victorious, you are overwhelmingly victorious, through Christ and the power of His love.

As mentioned in Challenge 3, my son is involved in wrestling. I know very little about the sport, but I do know one thing, there is a difference between winning and pinning. In wrestling you can win by scoring more points than your opponent. This can be a long process that can take the full length of three matches. It requires precision and technique, but mostly you must outlast your opponent. Then, there is "winning by pinning" your opponent. That is where you get them down on the mat and overwhelm them with strength and power.

My son had matches where he barely won. There have been wrestling matches that went the entire three rounds of nail-biting battle parlaying as he tried as hard as he could to get his opponent down— scoring points, losing points—to have a judge raise his hand in the end as victorious.

My son also had matches where in the first moments he exploded in power and overwhelmed his opponent, knocking them down and winning within seconds. In one match he conquered, in the other match he was more than a conqueror.

Now, a win is a win, but what Paul is saying is that in Christ Jesus, you don't have to just simply win. You don't have to simply eke out a victory in your relationships, or eke out a victory in your finances.

He is saying that in Christ, and in the power of His love, you overwhelmingly win. You can dominate with such fierce strength that it testifies not only to your lasting power, but to the overwhelming power of His might at work in and through you.

I love it, because God does not just want your life to be a win, He wants it to be such an overwhelming win that the world around you stops and takes notice. That is a powerful win!

We know that we are at war. Not a war with flesh and blood, but with powers and principalities, against anything that tries to exalt itself against God. (Ephesians 6:12) Earlier in Romans, Paul tells us that the enemy is trying to take us out, using tactics to get his own win: trouble, hardship, persecution, famine, nakedness, and the sword. These are real attacks of the enemy similar to those many of us may deal with daily.

Paul is saying that God gets it, He understands, but these things have no power in your life. Not only do they have no victory over you, but in all these things you are more than a conqueror. That is the assurance you have that no matter what comes your way today, you already have the victory. That gives you the assurance that today you are already victorious.

Understanding that you are victorious gives you a boldness and confidence that will change the way you live your days. Partnering with God's love brings peace, joy, strength, and a hope that empowers you to live abundantly. God wants you to partner with His power to live victoriously, in every area of your life.

That is the power of the victory that we have in Christ. He is the power for living a life that is truly victorious in Him!

Challenge: Consider, then write down your responses:

1. What is the biggest revelation you have received about yourself through this book?
2. What has changed in your thinking or beliefs since you began on Challenge 1?

3. How has your prayer life changed?

4. In what ways are you able to live more victoriously?

5. What has God shown you about His nature and character in the last 21 Challenges?

Prayer: "Heavenly Father, I thank You and give You praise because You are a good God who is madly in love with me. I thank You that You have pursued me, redeemed me, and restored me. Thank You that nothing can ever separate me from Your love. Today I celebrate the victories that I have had, walk in today, and will have in You. Because of Your love, fear has no power in my life, doubt has no authority in my life, and worry has no influence in my life. I press wholly and fully in to the power of the victory I am assured of in and through Your unquenchable love. No matter what comes my way, I know that in You, I am more than a conqueror. Today, I choose to live VICTORIOUSLY! In Jesus' name, Amen."

YOUR VICTORY

VICTORIOUS

ABOUT THE AUTHORS

Matthew and Siobhan Oliver are partners in ministry, business and life. They married after meeting in Bible College at the Brownsville Revival School of Ministry 18 years ago. They have been serving in ministry ever since - currently as Senior Pastors at The Family Church in Roseville, California. They strongly believe that church is more than just what goes on during a Sunday morning; church happens where life happens. Their heart is for everyone, everywhere to be able to meet a good, loving God.

Matthew and Siobhan are big dreamers, who are passionate about life, strong in their faith, and courageous in their love for God, people, and their regional community. In addition to owning two local businesses, they are involved in local theater, community sports, PTC, non-profits, and charities.

They reside in Rocklin, CA, with their three youngest children.

Matthew has also written *Taking Back the Night*, *40 Days of Greatness*, and co-authored *40 Days to a Healthy Heart*, with Sami Kader.